Contents

Introduction 1

The skills and knowledge needed for talking 2

The principles of the programme 2
    Improving everyday communication 2
    Targeting the specific profile of needs 4
    Working on speech, language and communication skills in parallel 6
    Recording progress and planning 6
    The DownsEd checklists 6

Interactive communication 9
    Developing early communication skills - some hints for parents and carers of babies ... 9
    Games to encourage attention - listening and looking 9
    Joint attention - looking and listening together 11
    Developing intentional communication 11

Signing 14

Conversational skills 18

Speech 19
    Speech sounds 21

Teaching vocabulary 31
    Choosing vocabulary to teach 31
    Games for vocabulary learning 32
    Teaching first words 34
    Two words 41
    Three words together 44

Grammar needs to be taught 44
    Syntax and grammar 45

Overview 50

Speech and language therapy 50

References 52

Speech and language

Speech and language development for infants with Down syndrome (0-5 years)

Sue Buckley and Gillian Bird

Summary - This module provides a programme of activities and advice designed to assist the development of speech and language skills for children with Down syndrome from birth to five years. The advice and activities are based on knowledge of the processes affecting speech and language development in typically developing children, the identified difficulties of children with Down syndrome and current research findings from studies evaluating effective remedial strategies. It also includes checklists for evaluating and recording children's development of interactive communication skills, speech sounds, vocabulary, sentences and grammar. The programme will enable parents, teachers and therapists to help children with Down syndrome to learn to talk, to talk in sentences, and to develop their speech clarity and conversational skills. It starts with activities to develop the foundation skills in infancy that lead on to talking, including the use of gesture and sign to support comprehension, and with an emphasis on speech sound work from infancy. Building a spoken vocabulary to 400 words by 5 years of age is seen as a priority, in order to develop grammar and phonology, and a recommended vocabulary programme with record sheets is included. The ways in which reading activities should be used to support all aspects of speech and language learning during preschool years are mentioned but the detailed advice on teaching early reading is in the reading module. This module follows on from *Speech and language development for individuals with Down syndrome - An overview* [DSii-03-01] which should be read first, to provide the reader with an adequate understanding of speech and language development to be successful in using this programme.

Series Editors

Sue Buckley and Gillian Bird

DSii-03-02-(en-gb) (January, 2001)

http://www.down-syndrome.info/library/dsii/03/02/

First published: January, 2001

Revision: 1.02

ISBN: 1-903806-05-4

A publication of The Down Syndrome Educational Trust

The Sarah Duffen Centre, Belmont Street, Southsea,
Hampshire, PO5 1NA, United Kingdom.

Telephone	+44 (0)23 9285 5330
Facsimile	+44 (0)23 9285 5320
E-mail	enquiries@downsed.org
Web Site	http://www.downsed.org/

The Down Syndrome Educational Trust is a charity, registered in England and Wales (number 1062823).

Proceeds from this publication support future research, services and publications. The production of this book provides employment for adults with Down syndrome.

The rights of Sue Buckley and Gillian Bird to be identified as authors of this Work has been asserted by them in accordance with sections 77 and 78 of the Copyright, Designs and Patents Act 1988.

Copyright © The Down Syndrome Educational Trust 2001. All Rights Reserved.

No part of this publication may be reproduced, or transmitted, in any form or by any means, or stored in a retrieval system of any nature, without the prior written permission of the publisher. Any person who does any unauthorised act in relation to this publication may be liable to criminal prosecution and civil claims for damages.

This book is sold subject to the condition that it shall not, by way of trade or otherwise, be lent, re-sold, hired out or otherwise circulated without the publisher's prior consent in any form of binding or cover other than that in which it is published and without a similar condition including this condition being imposed on the subsequent publisher.

Concept and design: Frank Buckley.

Typeset, printed and distributed by a wholly-owned subsidiary of The Down Syndrome Educational Trust:

DownsEd Limited
The Sarah Duffen Centre, Belmont Street,
Southsea, Hampshire, PO5 1NA.
United Kingdom.

Authors

Sue Buckley
Emeritus Professor of Developmental Disability, Psychology Department, University of Portsmouth, UK
Director of Research and Training, The Down Syndrome Educational Trust, UK.

Gillian Bird
Director of Consultancy and Education, The Down Syndrome Educational Trust, UK.

With contributions by Patricia Le Prevost and Gilly Haslegrave, adapted from earlier joint-authored publications.

Acknowledgements

The authors would like to thank all of the children, families and colleagues that they have had the privilege to work with and learn from over a period of 20 years. In particular, they would like to record their thanks to Patricia Le Prevost, Specialist Speech and Language Therapist, who provided most of the games illustrated and from whom they have learned a great deal that they hope is accurately reflected in this publication.

The authors would also like to thank Patricia Le Prevost, Ben Sacks and Leela Baksi for their helpful comments on various drafts of this module and the checklists. However, the responsibility for the final content, and any errors, is solely that of the authors.

Terminology

The term 'learning difficulty' is used throughout this module as it is the term currently in common use in the United Kingdom. The terms 'mental retardation', 'intellectual impairment', and 'developmental disability' are equivalent terms, used in other parts of the world.

In this module, the authors have adopted a straightforward and direct style in which the reader is addressed in the first person. They have done this because the module is mainly concerned with practical activities and instructions, and the authors have found that this direct, active style has been appreciated by readers in previous publications.

Speech and language development for infants with Down syndrome from birth to 5 years

Introduction

The main aim of this module is to provide practical advice and activities to improve the spoken language of children with Down syndrome. The focus is therefore on learning to understand and to use words and sentences and on developing the sound production skills necessary to produce intelligible speech.

Since babbling and early non-verbal communication using gesture and sign, are important and influence the rate of language learning in children with Down syndrome, sections on these are included but the emphasis in this module is on teaching vocabulary and developing sound discrimination and production. The aim is to help each child to develop a *spoken* vocabulary as quickly as possible and to acquire 400 words or more, used in sentences, by five to six years of age. There is evidence that this vocabulary size is necessary for the development of grammar and sentence structures and for control over speech sound production (phonology).[DSii-03-01 p.10] Signs are used with words to accelerate early word comprehension and effective communication, particularly as a bridge to the first 50 to 100 words. When a child has 50 words in his/her signed or spoken vocabulary, reading activities are encouraged to develop the production of two and three words together, early grammar and sentences.

The advice and programme of activities recommended in this module are based on three sets of information

- research into the processes and influences on speech and language development in typically developing children
- research into the specific speech and language needs of children with Down syndrome
- research into effective interventions
- the extensive experience of the authors' and other colleagues from working with parents to provide interventions

Speech and language development for infants with Down syndrome

A set of checklists, covering speech, vocabulary, grammar and interactive communication skills, is provided with this module to allow children's skills in each area to be evaluated, the activities to be targeted at the right level and to record progress.

The skills and knowledge needed for talking

For all children, learning to talk is a complex process, involving a number of emerging skills, influenced by learning opportunities and accomplished over many years. To be competent at expressing themselves through language, children have to know the words and grammar needed to express their thoughts in spoken language (language knowledge), they have to be able to make the sounds and words clearly so that their speech can be understood (speech) and they have to know how to engage someone effectively in a conversation (interactive communication skills). The reader is referred to the Speech and Language overview module for a full discussion of these issues and the key findings from research for both typically developing children and children with Down syndrome.

> **See also:**
> - Speech and language for individuals with Down syndrome - An overview [DSii-03-01]

Table 1. The skills and knowledge needed for talking

Interaction	Spoken language knowledge		Speaking
Non-verbal skills smiling, eye-contact, taking turns, initiating a conversation, maintaining the topic (pragmatics, discourse skills)	**Vocabulary** building a dictionary of single words and their meanings (lexicon and semantics)	**Grammar** learning the word ending rules for plurals, tenses, word order rules for questions, negatives, (morphology and syntax)	**Speech/motor skills** learning to make speech sounds, produce clear words with correct stress and intonation (articulation, phonology and prosody)

The principles of the programme

The programme is based on two main principles: The need to improve the quality and quantity of everyday communication with the child, and the need to target the specific skills that underpin effective communication as many of these skills are areas of particular difficulty for children with Down syndrome.

To maximise the child's speech and language progress *both everyday communication experience and the child's underlying skills* need to be considered at all times, for babies and children with Down syndrome.

We then stress two additional principles: The need, at all ages, to develop interactive communication, speech and language skills in parallel, and the importance of keeping records of progress.

Improving everyday communication

It is essential that everyone involved with a child with Down syndrome at home or school or in the community considers and, if necessary, improves the way in which they are communicating with the child during ordinary activities.

Learning to talk is an everyday activity.

Language is learned because children want to communicate and the single most important influence on the rate of progress in typically developing chil-

> **To improve the speech and language skills of children with Down syndrome you need to:**
> - Improve the quality and quantity of everyday communication with the child
> - Target the skills that underpin effective communication - many of these are areas of specific difficulty for children with Down syndrome
> - Work on interactive communication, language and speech in parallel
> - Record progress

dren is the quality and quantity of communication that the child experiences throughout their day at home or at school.

Therefore, one approach to language intervention is to encourage everyone who is with the child to be sensitive to the way in which they communicate with the child and to increase the amount of quality daily talk with the child.

Therapy based on quality interaction

The Hanen programme,[1] which teaches parents or carers about how language is learned by most children – the stages and the processes – and aims to improve the adult's sensitivity to the child's language learning needs, is one example of this approach. Intervention programmes that focus on interaction and language aim to improve the effectiveness of parents, teachers and carers as language teachers, during all their ordinary everyday communication with the child.

Of course, many parents, teachers and carers are excellent natural communicators and they adapt to the child's needs without any further training. However, communication is a two way activity between partners and when one partner is having difficulty, and does not give natural, age appropriate responses during the communication exchange, then it is not certain that all adults or other children will adapt to this as effectively as they could without some explicit guidance and conscious effort.

For example, if the child does not begin to point or hold up objects at the typical age, this may result in parents naming objects for the child less often, so delaying vocabulary learning. If the child does not begin to try saying words at the typical age, it may not be as easy to keep up the same level of talk to the child as it would be to the child who is talking and is demanding a response. If the child's words are unintelligible, the adult may need to ask the child to repeat the words, to be sure they understand what the child is trying to say, before they can respond. This disrupts the normal flow of conversation and the adult's ability to respond to the child's message by expanding or replying in a natural way.

All these examples indicate that when a child has even one area of delay or difficulty in her/his speech and language skills, this will almost certainly reduce the quality and quantity of natural talk to and with the child, in comparison with a typically developing child. Yet the child with difficulties needs *more* good quality language experience and learning opportunities than the typical child in order to make progress.

The first requirement for any parent, teacher or carer using this programme is that you are familiar with the stages of speech and language development in typically developing children and with what is currently understood about the processes that influence their rate of progress. In particular you should be confident that you know what skills and style of communication will make you a good communicator. You can do this by reading the overview module in this series and other books from the recommended list at the end of this module. You can also do this by learning from your local speech and language therapy service or from going on a course.

The second requirement is that you should then take time to consider how you are currently communicating with your baby or child with Down syn-

Speech and language development for infants with Down syndrome

drome and identify ways in which you could improve either your style or the quantity of communication experience that you are offering the child.

The third requirement is that, as you read in the next section about the additional ways that you can help your child, you remember that they are *additional*, they do not conflict with any of the principles which make you a good communicator. Some require you to try to absorb them and use them in all your everyday interactions to make all your communication with your child more effective (for example, speaking clearly, reducing background noise, maintaining eye contact, using signs). Others require some time to be spent each day on extra games and teaching activities. Try to absorb some of these activities into times when you already play with your child (during changing, bathing, bedtime and mealtimes, for example). Others can be included in no more than an a half hour session each day of planned playing or reading activities with your child (or two 15 minute sessions). In school the teaching games can be easily absorbed into the current programme of the nursery, preschool or classroom. Fifteen minutes of planned activities *daily* really will make a difference – and be more effective than an hour twice a week.

Targeting the specific profile of needs

Children with Down syndrome usually experience considerable delay and difficulties with learning to talk. Current research, described in the accompanying speech and language overview module, identifies a common profile.

Most children and adults with Down syndrome understand more language than their expressive language skills suggest and therefore their understanding is often underestimated. Their social interactive skills and non-verbal communication skills are a strength but speech sound production (articulation and phonology) is a specific weakness. Vocabulary learning, while delayed, is also a strength but grammar learning is a weakness, so that the children tend to talk using keywords rather than complete sentences.

Children with Down syndrome show the same progression from one word to two word combinations, once they can say between 50-100 words, as other children, and they show the same progression to early grammar in their speech when they have a spoken vocabulary of 300-400 words. Unfortunately the usual delay in reaching a productive vocabulary of 300-400 words (at 5 to 6 years, instead of at 2 to 3 years) may compromise the ability to master fully sophisticated grammar and phonology in later speech.

Progress in comprehension and production of vocabulary is probably compromised by hearing difficulties. It is certainly compromised by the children's specific difficulty with speech sound production. Progress in sentence production and in later grammar learning is probably compromised by a weakness in the auditory or phonological short-term memory system.

This profile of strengths and weaknesses identifies that any remedial programme needs to aim to:

1. Reduce the effects of hearing loss by:

a. Regular hearing assessments and prompt, effective surgical and/or medical treatments

b. Reducing background noise, speaking clearly and maintaining eye-contact while speaking

---

Summary of the speech and language profile of individuals with Down syndrome

- Speech and language skills are specifically delayed relative to non-verbal abilities
- Non-verbal communication is a strength in infancy and beyond
- Use of gestures to communicate is a strength
- Vocabulary is understood slowly but steadily and becomes a strength
- Spoken production of words lags behind comprehension
- Early grammar is learned slowly and is paced by vocabulary size
- More complex grammar is specifically delayed relative to vocabulary
- Spoken production of grammar lags behind comprehension of grammar
- Difficulty with speech production – first words delayed, strings of words difficult
- Articulation and phonology are a challenge, therefore speech intelligibility is a weakness
- Teenagers and adults often still communicate with short, telegraphic sentences

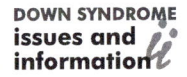

Speech and language development for infants with Down syndrome

Some of the reasons for the speech and language difficulties

- Learning difficulties - need more examples to learn
- Anatomical differences - affect speech skills
- Learning language from listening is affected by:
  - hearing loss
  - auditory discrimination
  - verbal short-term memory
- Speech motor difficulties:
  - delay vocabulary and grammar development
  - affect the way a child is talked to and included in conversations
- Joint attention difficulties and slow development of speech will both reduce language learning opportunities

All these difficulties can be targeted with appropriate and effective intervention strategies

    c. Using compensating strategies in the child's communication environment which make maximum use of visual supports (signs, pictures, print)

2. Improve articulation and phonology by:

a. Encouraging control over oral motor skills from infancy
b. Building up sound discrimination and production skills at babble stage
c. Practising single speech sounds from 12-18 months
d. Keeping a record of the child's speech sound skills
e. Practising whole word and sentence production
f. Using signs and reading activities to support speech sound work

3. Accelerate vocabulary comprehension and production by:

a. Teaching a target vocabulary
b. Keeping a record of the child's comprehension and production of words
c. Using an augmentative communication system, usually signs, to support comprehension and production of words
d. Using reading activities to support the comprehension and production of vocabulary

4. Accelerate mastery of grammar and sentence building by:

a. Teaching the use of two, three and four word combinations
b. Teaching the early grammatical markers (bound morphology)
c. Teaching word order rules (syntax)
d. Teaching function word grammar (closed class grammar)
e. Keeping a record of the child's comprehension and production of grammatical markers and sentences
f. Using reading activities to support the comprehension and production of grammar and sentences

5. Take account of the auditory short term memory weakness by:

a. Practising words to improve the sound traces stored
b. Playing memory games
c. Supporting learning with visual materials, pictures and print, to reduce memory requirement

6. Capitalise on the children's good social interactive skills and develop them by:

a. Being sensitive to all the child's attempts to communicate, by listening and responding to them
b. creating opportunities for the child to make choices and to express him/herself through language
c. Encouraging the use of gesture to communicate as it is a strength and may be important throughout life for some individuals
d. Remembering to listen and to wait to give the child a chance to organise their contribution to the conversation

e. Using styles of conversation that encourage the child to expand on and develop their contribution

f. Providing as many social opportunities for the child to be able to communicate with and learn from other non-language delayed children and adults in ordinary classes, clubs and social activities as possible

Working on speech, language and communication skills in parallel

Whenever we communicate we are using all these skills, right from infancy, therefore at any age an effective speech and language therapy programme needs to consider the child's strengths and weaknesses in communication, language knowledge and in speech. The programme should then work on each aspect as necessary, in parallel, rather than concentrate on language learning and neglect speech, for example.

Recording progress and planning

We believe that it is important to keep records of the child's progress as this:

- Encourages careful observation and an accurate knowledge of the stage the child has reached in each area of development
- Provides a record of progress and achievements
- Provides a guide to the next skill or step forward that is to be expected, allowing you to choose the next activity to focus on with confidence that your child should be ready to move towards it
- Ensures that the child's skills are not underestimated
- Keeps parents and teachers on task and motivated

We do not wish to impose too much extra work for families, teachers and carers but the evidence does suggest that speech and language skills need additional targeted help and that most children and adults with Down syndrome could be talking more and talking more clearly if we take relatively simple but planned steps to help them.

Learning to talk is the most important thing that children do. It is central to all other aspects of their development. It is critically important for social and emotional development and for the development of cognitive or mental abilities, so progress with learning to talk will benefit every other aspect of a child's life.

The DownsEd checklists

The Down Syndrome Educational Trust has developed a set of checklists to allow you to evaluate your child's current speech, language and communication skills and to record future progress in a simple and straightforward manner. The checklists cover interactive communication and play skills, speech sound skills, vocabulary and sentences and grammar.

For vocabulary, three lists are provided to take your child to an 800-word vocabulary in stages, the first 120, then the next 340 and the remaining 350. The words chosen are based on research on the order in which children learn words. The third list also includes the key vocabulary required for reading and for number in the first year or two in school and the words needed to

See also:

- *Vocabulary checklists and record sheets: Checklist 1 - First 120 words* [DSra-01-01]
- *Vocabulary checklists and record sheets: Checklist 2 - Second 340 words* [DSra-01-02]
- *Vocabulary checklists and record sheets: Checklist 3 - Third 350 words* [DSra-01-03]
- *Speech sounds checklists and record sheets* [DSra-02-01]
- *Interactive communication and play checklists and record sheets* [DSra-03-01]
- *Sentences and grammar checklists and record sheets* [DSra-04-01]

develop more advanced grammar and sentence structures. Remember that it is important that your child masters a 300-400 word spoken vocabulary as soon as possible as research evidence indicates that this is necessary before grammar will develop and that it will promote development of speech production skills. However, the learning difficulties of children with Down syndrome vary widely, therefore what really matters is that your child is progressing, even in small steps, and that communicating together is fun and effective.

The speech sounds checklist covers all 44 single sounds (phonemes) used in English and the common blends and clusters. The sentences and grammar

Table 2. Typical production milestones for children with Down syndrome

Age	Interaction	Vocabulary	Grammar	Speech
0-12 months	Crying Eye-contact Smiling Listening/looking Vocalising - coos Turn taking	Understanding words		Babble Babble tuned to native language
12-24 months	Joint attention Gestures Conveying an increasing number of meanings in gestures and some words	Beginning to sign Beginning to say words First 10 words		Initial consonants and vowels developing as single sounds
24-36 months	Initiating conversations - pointing, requesting	First 30 words Comprehension ahead of production	Two words together	Words not very clear/intelligible
36-60 months	Repairing conversations when not understood - by trying again	First 100 words Rate of word learning increases At 5 years about 300 words	Two and three key words together Early grammar begins	Consonant, vowel and word production improve in accuracy
5-7 years	Learning to tell short narratives	Vocabulary learning continues to accelerate At 7 years about 400 words	'Telegraphic' sentences - keywords Increasingly correct short sentences	Consonant and vowel production continue to improve in accuracy
7-16 years	Taking part in longer topic related conversations Requesting clarifications using - What?, Where? Telling stories Developing social use of language further - social small talk Taking account of listener's knowledge, knowing how to provide appropriate amounts of information for person or social situation Giving longer explanations or instructions Telling jokes Recounting experiences	More new words are learned each year Typical vocabulary size of older children and teenagers not known	Correct syntax being mastered slowly More difficult prepositions ... 'above', 'below' conjunctions - 'and', 'then', 'because' comparatives - 'longer than' Grammar steadily extended to include passives in comprehension Many of these features are learned and used in reading and writing and then in speaking	Blends improve Speech becomes steadily more intelligible Speech rate and speech clarity continue to improve, influenced by reading

Speech and language development for infants with Down syndrome

checklist gives examples of the early two and three word combinations that children use and then provides a guide to developing grammar.

The interactive communication and play skills checklist provides a guide to the range of communicative functions that children use, and to their ability to join in and initiate conversations. It also covers imaginative play activities as they demonstrate a child's growing understanding of the world and this can indicate the words and phrases that the child is ready to use.

The set of checklists are a guide to all aspects of speech and language development and communication skills for children with Down syndrome from birth to five years. Some of the skills that they cover will not be mastered by most children until they are into school, so the checklists will be a useful guide to be used over a number of years.

They are designed to allow children's progress to be carefully monitored and to ensure that activities are selected that are appropriate to advance children to the next step in development. The checklists are provided with the practical speech and language modules in this series and the speech and language overview module. They are intended to be used in conjunction with the information in those modules. However, the checklists are also available for purchase in sets for school, group, or speech and language therapy services.

Using the checklists

Before you start choosing activities from those given in this module, we suggest that you observe your child over the next few days and note down the gestures, signs and words that he/she is already using to communicate. If your child is already joining words together, then note down the words that he/she is using during the day. Keep an observation diary close to hand and write the words down just as they are said – for example 'juice, mum' or 'go school bus' or 'me car'. Make a note of the range of communication that your child engages in, for example, showing, asking, refusing or greeting. You will be able to use your observations to complete the checklists and decide on the correct targets for your child.

Remember we are all experts at language

The checklists and all the information in this and the overview module may seem daunting. When we analyse how we learn to talk and break it down into interactive skills, sounds, words and grammar, we make it seem complicated. We hope that the detail does help you to understand all the skills that your child is mastering step by step – but do remember that you are a competent talker and communicator and that you do use all the grammar described and the speech sounds, naturally. When some of the ideas seem difficult, just think about how you talk and you will see how you use tenses, prepositions and pronouns and auxiliary verbs, for example, without usually having to think about them.

Getting started

The activities are set out for each area of development starting with interactive communication skills, gesture and sign, then speech, vocabulary and grammar. In each area, activities are recommended in developmental order, so remember to identify your child's achievements in each area and choose activities to help her/him to progress in each area. It is important to recog-

See also:
- *Vocabulary checklists and record sheets: Checklist 1 - First 120 words [DSra-01-01]*
- *Vocabulary checklists and record sheets: Checklist 2 - Second 340 words [DSra-01-02]*
- *Vocabulary checklists and record sheets: Checklist 3 - Third 350 words [DSra-01-03]*
- *Speech sounds checklists and record sheets [DSra-02-01]*
- *Interactive communication and play checklists and record sheets [DSra-03-01]*
- *Sentences and grammar checklists and record sheets [DSra-04-01]*

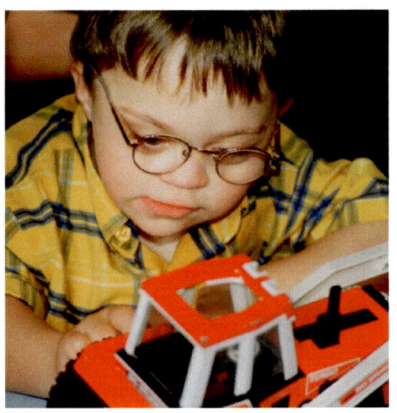

nise that the checklists cover at least five years of development. You do not need to read the whole of the module and take in all the advice and ideas at once. Start by completing the checklists and reading the sections that will provide activities for the next steps, based on your child's current level of progress.

Interactive communication

Interactive communication skills are usually a strength for children and adults with Down syndrome. Most children and adults want to communicate and to participate in social situations. They use and understand the non-verbal communication skills that everyone uses including eye-contact, smiling, facial expressions and gesture to communicate and to support spoken communication, right from infancy. They also use both verbal and non-verbal skills for the same range of communicative functions as everyone else, even though they may not be able to express themselves as fluently in speech as their non-disabled peers.

Interactive communication skills include all the non-verbal skills identified, which are used from the first year of life, and they include the conversational skills that develop later as children become competent talkers, such as telling stories and initiating conversations with visitors.

In infancy, it is important to encourage all forms of communication because early non-verbal skills, including gestures, lead to spoken language and also because children with Down syndrome may rely on non-verbal skills for longer than other children.

Developing early communication skills – some hints for parents and carers of babies

Encouraging eye-contact, smiling, singing, babbling, using appropriate facial expression and talking to babies from the first month of life will help to develop early communication skills. Respond to your baby's feelings or emotional states as you would for any other baby, but be aware that your baby may not have such loud or clear communication, so do try to attribute meaning to their movements or efforts, even when you are not really sure what he/she is trying to express. Show your enjoyment of playing with him/her, encouraging your baby to watch and listen and enjoy interacting with you.

Follow your baby's lead as much as possible and talk about what the baby is doing, looking at or playing with. Give your baby time to organise her/his response, as babies with Down syndrome may take a little longer to react than typically developing babies. At first, your baby will look at you and other faces as the main source of interest and entertainment, and then later in the first year of life will show interest in other visual, auditory and moving things – this is the stage when joint attention becomes possible and you can name what the baby is looking at or doing.

Games to encourage attention - listening and looking

Looking and listening are very important skills, which are needed for learning to understand and use language, and should therefore be encouraged.

Speech and language development for infants with Down syndrome

Games to encourage looking

Attract your baby's attention by clapping your hands, calling her/his name or shaking a rattle, then praise the baby when he/she looks at you. Once you have your baby's attention, try and hold it for as long as possible by talking, babbling, (playing with sounds), smiling, pulling faces and praising the baby as he/she responds. If your baby begins to copy your facial movements or sounds keep encouraging her/him. Feeding and bathing are good times for gaining and maintaining eye contact with your baby. Hang bright objects or mobiles over your baby's cot and encourage her/him to look at them by shaking them. Then put them near enough so if the baby moves a hand he/she will touch them and move them.

Gain your baby's attention by holding a brightly coloured object in front of her/him, then move it slowly to one side and encourage the baby to follow it with her/his eye gaze. Move objects away from the baby and see if he/she grabs for them.

Toys that produce sounds or movement are interesting for infants. Using, for example, a 'jack in the ball', or 'jack in the box', encourage the child to look at the box or the ball then hold his attention for a few seconds, press the button and the 'jack pops up' (a good intrinsic reward). A baby mat on the floor with mirrors, rattles and toys attached may encourage your baby to attend and to begin to explore toys for her/himself.

Play 'peek-a-boo' and 'round and round the garden' games to help gain attention and eye contact.

In addition to encouraging eye contact and communication, these games will increase your baby's attention span. This is important, as your baby needs to be able to attend and concentrate for increasingly long periods of time in order to learn, as he/she gets older. In our experience, this is a problem for some children with Down syndrome, who find it difficult to sit still and attend. We find that children who have been played with from infancy, and expected to attend to games and to books for example, have longer attention spans and are better able to cooperate in learning situations at two or three years of age and later, in the classroom.

Games to encourage listening

A variety of games can be played to encourage listening and sound discrimination. Give your baby a rattle to shake, join in with your own rattle and when the baby shakes her/his, you shake yours, stop when the baby stops and then start again when he/she does. You could try this the other way round. You start by shaking the rattle and see if your baby joins in. If he/she does, then continue rattling then stop and see if he/she stops. Use different noise makers to attract your baby's attention, squeaky toys or perhaps your own home made ones, e.g. rice or dried peas in different containers. Move the noise makers away and see if the baby reaches for them. Move them slightly to one side and see if the baby follows with her/his eyes. Show your baby a noise maker, shake it then hide it under a rug or in a box still shaking it and see if he/she looks

Figure 1. Everyday sounds game
Collect suitable pictures, place the cards face down, make the sound and ask the child to turn the card, saying "What makes this sound? Brrrm.. Brrrm... It's a bus! Let's make a bus sound." End with the balloon card, saying "It's a balloon and the balloon goes Pop!" as you and the child/children clap hands. (The children enjoy waiting for the balloon pop).

for it. See if your baby turns her/his head as you move the sound maker away to one side.

Draw your baby's attention particularly to household noises, e.g., a clock ticking, a spoon stirring in a cup, running tap water, telephone ringing, kettle boiling, etc. Show the baby what is making the noise, talk about it, and tell her/him what it is. When your baby can sit, independently or supported, a good game for looking and listening is pushing a ball between yourself and your child. Before you push it to her/him, call your baby's name and show her/him the ball, telling the baby what it is. Then as the baby looks at you push the ball to her/him. Gain the baby's attention before he/she pushes the ball back to you if possible.

Joint attention – looking and listening together

As well as sharing attention together, looking at and engaging each other, encourage joint attention sessions (where you and your baby both look and listen to the same things, like a rattle, or food, or toy, a person or a picture) and try to keep the baby's attention on task to build up the length of time he/she can attend to an activity with interest or enjoyment.

As you play and interact with your baby, your baby's ability to attend, by listening and looking, increases, as does his/her ability to be flexible in redirecting attention from one thing to another. These skills also develop as your baby manipulates or makes things happen in his/her environment, with early toys or people.

Your baby needs to learn to attend to things long enough to learn from the situation, toy or activity, but not for so long that he/she misses opportunities for learning about all of the other things and people around her/him. Sharing attention and joint attention will develop the attending skills the baby needs for learning and communicating. The parent with a baby who is easily distracted can help him/her to look and listen for a little longer, and a parent with a baby that attends to one thing for rather too long (e.g., looking at or playing with own feet) can help him/her to enjoy and attend to a wider range of activities. It is doing these things together that helps to develop communication skills.

Developing intentional communication

As babies use their skills and understand how their behaviours affect others (by the responses that parents give) they learn to communicate their needs in increasingly specific and effective ways. They communicate by looking, crying, moving parts of their bodies, picking things up, and these develop into gestures, such as offering things, holding out their hand to request something, while also looking, either at you or at the thing or action they want. Then gestures become words as children learn to talk. For children learning to sign, gestures will become signs that enable them to communicate more clearly for a wide range of words, before they are able to say the words.

Understanding how to communicate underpins effective speech and language development and developing intentional communication skills provides the foundation for learning to talk.

Children begin to tell others what to do, using gestures that attract the attention of adults and redirects it towards objects or things they want. They also begin to share aspects of their experiences with adults, with mutual eye-to-

---

Joint attention is important for language learning

- Joint attention is when the infant and carer are attending to the same object or activity
- In this situation the carer tends to talk about what they are both attending to
- This helps the infant to '*see what you mean*' and encourages comprehension of words and sentences
- Children who experience more joint attention episodes learn language faster

Speech and language development for infants with Down syndrome

eye contact and smiling, or by drawing the adult's attention to something by looking or pointing. Some of the types of things that young children communicate about are listed in the box (right).

The interactive communication skills checklist will enable you to record which of these intentions your child has and whether they use only early communicative behaviours (e.g., crying, laughing, looking), whether they also use gestures (e.g., moving their bodies, hands, arms, mouth in particular ways, shaking their head, pointing) or also say words (using simple sign and/or speech).

Gestures

As children begin to use more gestures, signs and sounds to communicate successfully, and learn that it is easier and more accurate to convey their needs or wishes using gestures, signs and early words, these will take over from earlier communicative behaviours. As they learn more words (or signs) these will replace the use of some gestures. Sometimes children use negative behaviours to communicate their needs, such as – moving away, throwing a tantrum or even just smiling. These will be replaced by more positive, communicative behaviours if children are shown or taught these more sophisticated skills, by seeing how others use them and copying them, and finally using them spontaneously to communicate their needs.

The development of communication skills is a gradual progression for all children, and your child can be helped along this developmental pathway – her/his communication skills are not unfolding in a predetermined way on a predetermined timescale, but are influenced by her/his interactions with others.

Learning to choose and point

Your child will learn how to become an intentional communicator with gestures by having these shown to him/her as you communicate together, as well as by the responses that you give to their efforts to communicate with you. Your child will also learn that he/she can have control over some aspects of daily life by being shown how to choose with encouragement to point, as well as to take items. Offer a choice of two items, for example, toys, activities, or foods, before starting an activity or meal. You will be able to judge from your child's response (look at, reach, push one away, hold in hand, indicate or touch with hand, point at) which one he/she prefers and this will motivate the child to use and develop his/her communication skills. If you can't judge a preference by the way the child looks or behaves, just choose the item he/she is actually looking towards at a moment in time and 'pretend' the child has chosen it, as this will help to develop his/her intentional communication skills. Looking at pictures and the reading of picture books together can also encourage pointing.

Imitating

Your child will learn by copying or imitating your actions, sounds or words. This takes time and your baby will watch an action or a sound at first, maybe for several weeks, before he/she imitates it. Be patient and keep up the games – you will be rewarded and thrilled when your baby begins to copy sounds, then actions and then words. Once your baby begins to actively imitate, he/she has taken a significant step forward in learning. Singing and action games are often the first stimulus to join in – starting with repeating

---

Intentional communication

- **Draws attention to self, events, objects or people** by vocalising and looking, coming close and leaning, tugging and pulling
- **Requests objects, actions, information or recurrence of actions** by reaching, putting your hand on item, by extended reach with open palm, gestures such as arms up to ask to be lifted up
- **Greeting** by hand out on vocalising, coming and hugging, waving bye-bye
- **Protests and rejects** by crying, pushing, stiffening, throwing, gesture
- **Gives information** by pointing, showing, giving, taking you to show you what has happened
- **Responds to Yes/No response** by vocalising, head nod for 'yes', head shake for 'no', by gesture.

Stages of language development

- Gestures
- Single words
- Two words together
- Longer keyword utterances
- Grammar – word endings and word order
- Grammar – function grammar
- Complete sentences

Speech and language development for infants with Down syndrome

Table 3. How communication progresses from gesture to words

Type of communication	1. Early skills e.g. crying, laughing, whole body posture, looking etc		2. Early skills and gesture e.g. looking and eye contact, moving head or arms, showing, giving, pointing etc		3. Early skills, gesture and use of words to communicate (signed or spoken)
Draws attention to self or others	e.g. crying, vocalising and looking, (or sometimes behaviours like throwing, banging), moving close to someone	+	social games, like blowing raspberries, hide and seek with head or eyes	+	signing and/or saying e.g. "me", or child's name (overlap with requests e.g. "me go", "my turn")
Draws attention to or comments about things	e.g. looks at or holds	+	showing, pointing at toys, pictures, activities, for you to share, acknowledge or talk about	+	name of item plus point, "look" or "what's that?"
Requests things	e.g. reaching for, holding, looking at, putting your hand towards	+	pointing, showing (as in box above) but also wanting things to be given or to happen, child may demonstrate the activity, e.g. arms up to be lifted, moving body or arms with excitements for an activity to be repeated, smacking lips to ask for more	+	signing and/or saying objects or activities name or description, e.g. "drink", "teddy", "up", "more", "again", "get it", "help"
Protests and rejects	e.g. crying, turning face away, pushing away, stiffening, throwing, refusal	+	head gesture for 'no'	+	signing or saying 'no'
Giving information	e.g. looking, crying, taking you to show you what has happened	+	pointing, showing, giving objects,	+	signing or talking about things and events, remembering about things that have happened
Expressing feelings	e.g. by crying, smiling, laughing, wriggling, screaming,	+	clapping, gesture for cuddle, smacking lips to indicate something tastes good, exaggerated face for dislike	+	signs and words, call mum/dad for cuddle, "go", "no like"
Absence	e.g. crying, looking for	+	shrugging to indicate 'all gone' or 'where did it go', pointing or taking to place something usually is or was previously	+	saying signs and words 'all gone', 'gone' or 'ball gone'
Greeting	e.g. looking, smiling	+	holds out arms, gestures hello, waving bye-bye	+	saying words 'hello' and 'bye'
Responds to yes/no response	e.g. by vocalising, crying,	+	head nod 'yes', by gesture, head shake 'no'	+	saying words

Speech and language development for infants with Down syndrome

actions such as 'clap hands' or 'peek-a-boo' – and then copying the words. One factor helping children to learn from these games may be the amount of repetition they experience, often playing the game everyday, several times a day. The same amount of repetition may be needed to learn ordinary words, which is why games to teach vocabulary are necessary to help children with Down syndrome.

Signing

The advantages of signing

It is important to use natural gestures with babies with Down syndrome from birth and to learn to use specific signs with words from 7 to 8 months of age. Gestures hold the baby's attention and help them to understand what is being said. It is important to understand that signs are to be used as a bridge to support the development of spoken language. The research evidence shows that children with Down syndrome do not learn words easily from speech input on its own and that those who have been in sign supported therapy programmes have bigger spoken vocabularies at 5 years.

All babies use signs such as pointing and waving, before they use words, so that in using more specific signs, we are extending a natural stage of development rather than introducing something that is not seen in typical development. Almost all children with Down syndrome will use spoken language as their main means of communication from 3 or 4 years onwards. The signs used to help them are keyword signs to support the learning of words. Signs are not being taught as a sign language, to be used instead of a spoken language, as might be the case for a deaf child. In particular, signs help children with Down syndrome to communicate effectively and show that they understand words at the stage when they cannot yet produce the sounds due to difficulties with speech production skills. This overcomes frustration and, most importantly, allows their comprehension of new words and therefore their cognitive (mental) development to proceed at a faster rate than if we waited for spoken words.

Practitioners have advocated the use of augmentative signing with babies with Down syndrome since the early 1980s and evidence for its effectiveness in accelerating both comprehension and production of language has accumulated steadily.

Signing can help babies and children to understand words in a number of ways.

If parents sign as they speak:-

- they make sure the baby is looking
- the sign holds the baby's attention
- the sign gives an added clue to the meaning of the words
- parents are also likely to stress the words they are signing and speak at a slower rate

In other words, signing may help to structure more effective language learning situations.

The benefits of using signs as a bridge to talking

- Children with Down syndrome are good at using gestures before they can talk
- Their first words are specifically delayed even when they understand early vocabulary
- Being able to sign allows them to communicate effectively and reduces frustration at this stage
- Parents who sign can engage in more effective language teaching and communication with their children
- Signs help children to understand and learn words - research shows that speech alone is not enough to teach new words
- Signs help children to be understood while their speech is still difficult to understand
- Children with Down syndrome have larger vocabularies when they have been in sign supported programmes
- Signs are a bridge to speaking and should be needed less as children learn to talk
- Speech sound work should be focused on from infancy alongside the use of signs
- The focus should always be on learning to say words, with signs used as an aid
- By school age signs should only be used as necessary and speaking should be the focus for daily communication

For infants, signing can increase their productive vocabularies as they can usually sign words before being able to say them - they know what they want to say but cannot yet produce the words.

At this stage, signing increases effective communication, and this enables language learning to continue at a greater rate until spoken language develops. Signing will reduce frustration and increase communication opportunities. However, it is essential to keep up activities to encourage sound and speech production alongside the use of signing, if children are to move into using spoken words as early as possible. In our experience, most children are able to drop the use of sign slowly from around four to five years of age, although they should not be discouraged from using sign at any age as a repair strategy when their speech is not understood and they will continue to benefit from the use of sign to teach new words and sentence structures.

How to begin to use signs – advice for parents

Remember that signs are being used as a natural support for your spoken words. If signs are used like gestures (and indeed many of them are just that) then they can explain to the baby what is being said or taught, and they are a means for the baby to tell you that he/she has understood or to ask for what he/she wants.

A very simple example of teaching gesture happens in every family when a parent is helping their child to say "good-bye." The parent takes the child's hand and, while waving it, says "wave bye-bye." The parent also imitates the action and 'waves bye-bye' as he/she says "bye-bye". Gradually the child copies and uses the action and in time says "bye-bye" too. There is never any thought that using the gesture first will stop the words from coming, or that it looks unnatural.

Signs are used in exactly the same way with children with Down syndrome, many of whom are not going to find the skills of speech easy, and therefore may need signs for longer – but success in communicating with sign encourages all children to try the words.

What are these signs, and how do we use them?

If you think of signs as an extension of the ordinary sort of gestures that you use every day, then you will not go far wrong. If you remember that you are signing to explain what your child is seeing in her/his little world, then you won't ask too much of either yourself or your child. As a baby, he/she will not need the ways of the whole world explained, such as the difference between a rhinoceros or a hippopotamus, but only the ways of her/his world. For example, your baby will want to be asked if he/she is thirsty, to be shown where the toys are, to know that he/she is going to have a bath, and that you are going to put socks on her/his feet. Your baby will love to point out the light to you and to listen when Grandma is on the phone. He/she may wish to watch the video, or eat an apple or banana, and your baby would like to tell you her/his choice (without having to scream in annoyance when you give her/him the wrong one!). Your baby will want to know when the other members of the family are coming home, and which of them is expected. Your baby will want a name for her/his favourite toy (even if it is a piece of blanket or a rather bedraggled toy!).

If you make sure that your baby can see what you are talking about, and that he/she does not have things just happen to her/him, if you point out where

Speech and language development for infants with Down syndrome

your baby's toy is on the floor before naming it and he/she is looking at it, then you will be doing a great deal to help the baby to learn. By adding the extra simple gestures/signs to explain daily life, then you are helping your baby even more.

Simple signing means:

- holding your hands out to show your baby that you are going to pick her/him up

- pointing to the light, and showing your baby how the light goes on, when he/she is looking at it.

- pretending to drink before you give her/him a drink so your baby knows what is coming.

- showing your baby a simple sign for 'cat' or 'dog' so that he/she can learn the name of the family pet.

- putting your hand to your ear when the phone rings so that your baby learns how to listen to it and its name.

- holding up your baby's sock and saying its name as you put it on so that he/she learns its name.

- putting you finger on your baby's nose, then your nose and asking your baby to do the same, as you say "nose".

These examples show that signing is about doing what you are doing already, but remembering that you are going to show your baby what is happening a bit more. By signing you are helping your baby to learn to *watch* for clues to the meaning of things in her/his world as well as to *listen*. As your baby learns to look to you for clues to her/his world, and to use signs, you will want to give your baby more information, and will therefore need to learn some more signs.

One of the most rewarding events is when your child can tell you that he/she not only understands what is going on, but can make her/his own comment about it. If your baby can use a sign to do so then the learning of the whole process of language has taken a great step forward. If you sign with your baby with Down syndrome then he/she will probably reach this point many months earlier than he/she could have done if relying on you understanding his speech.

Signs should always be used with natural speech, they are there to explain what you are saying and should never be used as an alternative to speech.

If they are used in this way, then they can be used as you would use any gesture, as naturally as possible. You don't want to have to think about how you are going to find the right gestures to explain your baby's world to her/him. There are books and courses to help you to learn signs, but you should choose signs based on what you think your child needs, and what you can use comfortably in your busy life. Having to stop and think how to 'talk' to your baby is difficult and could distort the natural way you talk to your baby. Choose a few signs at a time to use in your everyday communications to start with and add more as you feel at ease with signing. The book *See and Say* by Patricia Le Prevost[2] contains 150 signs and this is enough for early use. Other sign resources are listed at the end of the module.

Speech and language development for infants with Down syndrome

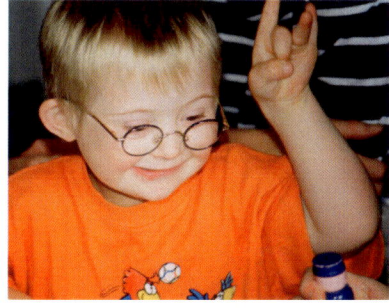
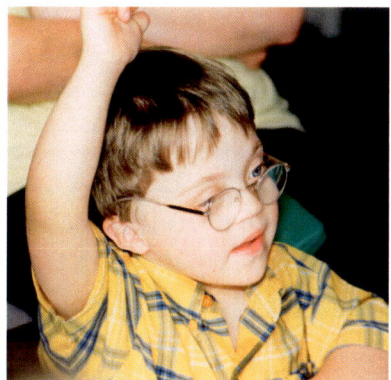

Early signs to use when talking to your baby

The first signs will support the things that you want to say to your child such as "hello", "up you come", "give me", "bye-bye", "all gone", "off we go", "what's that/this?", "do you want some more?", "look at (this)", "wait a minute", "where is it?", "(baby) do it", "good (boy/girl)", "put it there", "we're going to wash your (hands, face…)", and "night-night".

The next signs will be words that you are teaching your child to understand and say based on the vocabulary checklists such as "Mummy", "Daddy", "drink", "cup", "eat", "food", "biscuit", "crisp", "spoon", "bed", "car", "teddy", "home", "light", "telephone", "toys", "play", "no", "please", "I", "you", "we", "boy", and "girl".

In the authors' experience, most children with Down syndrome will not need to learn more than 50 to 100 signs before they are moving on to using words as their main means of communication. As they can begin to say a word, they usually drop the sign for that word and use the spoken word. This should be encouraged, as the spoken word will only become clearer with practice. However, sign can still support the learning of new vocabulary, as we know this will speed up learning to understand and use the new words.

Children will join signs together at the 'two-word' stage of language development and this is fine, but they should be encouraged to practice saying the words and reading the words. If children are still entirely dependent on signs when trying to put 2 and 3 words together, then their speech sound skills should be reviewed as they may be in need of extra help with speech sound production.

The use of sign at four years and older

By four years of age, the amount of signing a child needs will need to be judged on an individual basis. Some children will be moving to use speech confidently as their main mode of communication, others will still be dependent on signs and should be taught new signs. The critical issue will be the child's speech sound skills and spoken language, those with better

Speech and language development for infants with Down syndrome

sound production skills will be talking and those with more sound production difficulties and restricted vocabulary will need more signs. A speech and language therapist will be able to advise, but it is essential to take a careful look at the use of signing for each child. Speech is difficult for children with Down syndrome and their speech will only become clearer if they practice speaking. Few children with Down syndrome require a signing environment, where all spoken language is supported by signing, in the long term.

Used appropriately, with individual planning, signs continue to be an important aid at school age. Many individual case examples from parents and practitioners indicate that signing often helps the school age child with Down syndrome to find the word they want and to speak more clearly. Signs for sounds can help production of initial and end sounds in words and signs for grammatical markers can help to teach grammar.

However, it is essential that speaking is encouraged as the *main* mode of communication by four years of age and that every child is working on speech sounds. In our view, it is not appropriate to send every classroom assistant on a signing course because a child with Down syndrome is coming to the pre-school or school. Some children will be reading and talking and these should be the *main* modes of communication and they should be used to continue to promote their speech and language development. Other children will still be very dependent on sign and someone confident with an early signing vocabulary should support communication with them.

In summary, all children with Down syndrome benefit from the use of up to 100 signs, always used *with the spoken words*, to establish an early spoken vocabulary, but speech sound work must continue alongside the use of signs. The amount of signing that it is appropriate to use once a child understands and uses 100 or more words/signs needs to be judged on an individual basis. Signs used to support *new* words, sentences, sounds and grammar can help every child. In the authors' view, most children with Down syndrome should be encouraged to speak as their main mode of communication from four years of age, with reading as the main support system for learning new words and practising words and sentences. Too much use of unplanned signing when it is no longer necessary may hold back clear speech. However, a significant minority of four year olds (perhaps 25%) and older children will still need to use signs as their main mode of communication and should be taught new signs, alongside speech and reading work.

We suggest that parents may be the best judge of the sign/spoken word balance as they will know how best their child learns to understand new words and how best he/she communicates in everyday situations.

Conversational skills

As children become talkers and use their spoken language more confidently, we need to consider the way they are joining in and also starting conversations. If you ask a question, does your child respond? Does your child comment on things that he/she sees when you are out? Does he/she ask questions? Does he/she join in family conversation at the meal table? If not – is it possible to think of ways to include your child in family conversation and encourage him/her to ask questions. Initially, you may need to draw him/her into conversations by asking questions and then giving your child time to answer, followed by comments like 'that's interesting – and what else happened?' or 'can you tell me more?' You may need to take turns around

Speech and language development for infants with Down syndrome

the table, as this will provide your child with model sentences to copy and support him/her in taking a turn in the conversation.

You may also need to model, expect and prompt socially appropriate language at a level your child can master, for example "leave me alone, please" instead of "go away" or pushing. Some of the behaviours that seem inappropriate in young children at preschool are often used because the child cannot say what they want or what the problem is.

Be a good listener

Being interested in your child's activities and being a good listener really help in encouraging your child to talk and to share their experiences. However, it is not easy for children with Down syndrome to become fluent and confident in social situations and this issue will be addressed further in the module for 5-11 year olds.

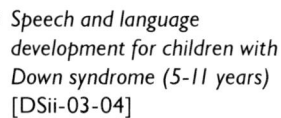

See also:
- Speech and language development for children with Down syndrome (5-11 years) [DSii-03-04]

Speech

From infancy activities that will lead to clear speech need to be a priority. Many aspects of the babies' development will have an influence on later speech skills, including breathing, feeding and drinking skills and general motor control.

In infancy

It is important to encourage good feeding, sucking, chewing, drinking and breathing habits from the first months of life. The coordination and control of the movement of lips, tongue and breathing needed for chewing and swallowing develops similar actions that are needed for making clear speech sounds. Therefore it is important to steadily move your baby on to chewing lumpy foods, just increasing the texture a little at a time until he/she can chew ordinary pieces of food. At the same time, move your baby forward from drinking from a bottle to a cup in stages, using a cup with a teat, then a spout, then a recessed lid and finally an ordinary cup. Some babies may not go through all these stages and find it easier to use a straw. Watch that you baby keeps her/his tongue inside the mouth when drinking, and does not put her/his tongue down the outside of the cup. Encourage your baby to learn to drink from a straw. The special straws with built-in valves, sold in the pharmacy, for those with difficulties such as stroke patients, can help. Encourage bubble blowing and whistle blowing games to get your baby to make a round lip closure.

Some babies seem to be hypersensitive and to dislike touch around the mouth area or the feel of things in and around their mouths and these children need help to tolerate these sensations. A specialist speech and language therapist can provide advice but if this is not available, gently massage your babies face with fingers, a face cloth, or a soft brush for a few minutes several times a day. Encourage the baby to try different tastes and textures and sometimes eating with fingers is more acceptable to the child than the feel of a spoon in their mouth.

Encourage mouth closure and nose breathing (use of dummy may help, but only when baby is not socialising and wanting to babble). Your baby's gross motor development, including head and trunk control and muscle tone, will also influence your baby's ability to control breathing and face, mouth and tongue muscles. Massaging you baby and encouraging her/him to enjoy kicking and splashing, during nappy changing and bath times, for example, will help to build up muscle tone and control.

A note on tube feeding

If your baby has been tube-fed during infancy, this may have affected the development of breathing, swallowing, chewing and muscle control. For this reason, tube-feeding should not continue for any longer than is absolutely essential. If your baby was tube-fed and you are concerned about her/his ability to chew or make sounds, seek expert help from a specialist in early oral-motor development through a paediatric or speech and language therapy service.

Encourage smiling and babbling

Smiling, babble games, and engagement with others will all keep the face mobile and active and exercise oral-facial muscles. Auditory discrimination training for speech sounds can begin early, in babble games and then in specific sound practice activities. Try to work on sounds, encouraging babies to copy sound and gesture from as early as possible, especially in babble games. Encourage babies to watch your lip movements - they can do this in face-to-face play and will copy the mouth shapes that they see. (Later you can do this sitting side by side in front of a mirror or when using sound cards). Singing games, working on words and sounds, can be fun and a good way to engage babies and toddlers.

Babble is important and sets the stage for later speech development. Babies practice speech sounds in their babble and they tune their babble to the particular sounds of the language that they are hearing by twelve months of age. The sounds that are contained in babies' babble lead to the first words that they will attempt to say. Interventions with sound work, which should later improve speech clarity, can therefore begin from the first weeks of life. This is the rationale for a system developed by Professor Irene Johansson in Sweden.[3] Parents can follow the programme themselves, although they will be helped greatly by an experienced speech and language therapist. This programme encourages parents to repeat different rhythms of sounds and syllables from early babyhood, with games and activities to teach children to make sounds, understand and use simple language and gestures. Some parents may find the full programme too intensive, but they may be able to adapt it and use the activities that they feel fit comfortably into their daily routines with the baby.

Natural play with your child will also encourage babble and copying, if you do not want to follow a programme. Imitation seems to be an important milestone, in gesture and in speech. Imitate your baby's sounds and babble, as well as encouraging particular new sounds, taking some of the initial sounds from the speech sounds checklist and introducing them to your baby.

See also:
- *Speech sounds checklists and record sheets* [DSra-02-01]

Babies move from babbling a variety of separate vowel and consonant sounds to producing repeated sounds such as 'baba' or 'dada'. This is setting the skills in place for trying easy words like "daddy" and "ball". Repeat and expand babble and first attempts at words. This is rewarding for the baby as he/she is taking part in a 'conversation' that they have initiated. The baby is also hearing a more accurate version of the sound or word they are trying and you are giving it meaning. Once the child begins to imitate, you can encourage practice. This will often lead to their first meaningful words as

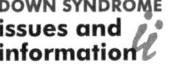

Speech and language development for infants with Down syndrome

you respond to babble as if it is a word and the baby realises the noise he/she is making does indeed mean something specific like "Daddy".

Speech sounds

Early sound games

Between the ages of 1 and 2 years young children with Down syndrome can be introduced to teaching activities that will help to develop their awareness of sounds and their ability to produce sounds through daily games. This type of work can be continued for as long as needed (and practice through talking and reading may take over), provided the activities are kept interesting and age appropriate for them. Activities that encourage the child, young person or adult to practice their sound and word production, with good models to copy and feedback, are effective for improving speech into adult life.

Pictures and signs help young children to remember sounds associated with those pictures and signs. Speech and language therapists in all countries have access to pictures, other materials and activities aimed at improving phonological awareness and speech production, although they may not know that these activities, designed primarily for children with speech and language disorders, are also appropriate for teaching children with Down syndrome. They may also not know how important it is for children with Down syndrome to begin learning through extra practice from their early years of life. Cued articulation[4] and the Nuffield Centre Dyspraxia Programme[5] are examples of this type of work. These and other programmes may not always be suitable for very young children though, and do require the guidance of a trained professional to advise when and how to introduce activities.

Sound cards

The Down Syndrome Educational Trust has published consonant sound cards and vowel sound practice cards, developed by Patricia Le Prevost, an experienced speech and language therapist who is recognised as an expert in working with children with Down syndrome. The cards encourage imitated consonant and vowel sound production and facilitate practice with gesture and pictures, and they can be used from about 18 months of age. The rationale is best explained in the information accompanying the sound cards.

When a baby is born, although the major concerns are those of survival, feeling comfortable, being well fed and warm, there is also the need to be in contact with others, and to feel safe and happy. One of the ways we express such feelings is through sounds. In a tiny baby, the early sounds are simple, but it is not long before patterns of sounds with rising and falling intonation patterns emerge.

Figure 2. DownsEd Sound Cards (fronts and backs)

The first sounds are mainly those made with the mouth open – "a-ah" and "e-e", etc. It is not long before other sounds, such as "d-d-d" and "m-m-m" are added. The baby is using the patterns of movement that are similar to sucking and are simpler versions of the ones we use in speech. As the muscles of the tongue get stronger, and the baby listens to all sounds his parents use when talking to her/him, so the range of sounds he/she produces gets larger. It is fun to play with these sounds not only when you are having a 'conversation' with someone,

Speech and language development for infants with Down syndrome

but also when you are on your own. Babies 'play' with sounds just as they play with their fingers and toes; it is a very good way to learn about making sounds.

Long before the first real words appear, babies realise that certain sounds joined together have a specific meaning. Babies practice the sounds that they hear around them over and over again. They will be able to make their tongues, lips, soft palates and vocal chords produce a wide variety of sounds, in fact, most of the sounds that occur in their own particular language. In the same way that a pianist has to practise in order to make his fingers move fast enough to play a piece of music at the correct speed, so every baby has to practise the wide variety of sounds that make up our speech. If the muscles of your mouth are not well coordinated (and that includes your tongue) then it is quite difficult to get fast movement as accurately as is needed for speech.

Babies love to play with sounds, but they will not develop the range of sounds needed for speech if they are finding the movements difficult, and will stick to sounds that are easy, such as all the vowel sounds. These make up the base upon which each word is built, but do not separate out one word from another. The tendency is also then, to stop listening to the soft sounds that change the meanings of words, so that 'eat', 'feet', 'see', 'read', etc all become "ee" with the meaning for each one distinguished by the context, just as we have to do for words such as 'see' and 'sea'.

Children may mix up these sorts of words while they are learning, and many others that sound similar, such as car and cart and card, and it is only by making mistakes and having them corrected (so they hear the correct pronunciation repeated back to them) that they learn the correct pronunciation and meaning.

The *DownsEd Sound Cards* work by giving parents the opportunity to introduce all the sounds in a way that is fun, while also helping their children to listen really well to each individual sound. The method is similar in principle to the methods used in remedial phonological training programmes for children and adults with Down syndrome (reviewed in the overview[DSii-03-01]).

Young children, beginning to use sound cards in play, are likely to look at the picture and the accompanying gesture or sign shown to them, and may begin to watch the way in which the mouth and tongue moves, while listening to the sound. After a number of sessions of looking, listening and playing with parents with the sound cards, children typically begin to join in with signing the sounds, followed by remembering and using the sign associated with the sound and picture, and finally, they copy and say the sound. The sounds may not be clear at first, but they should be praised and encouraged as the more children practice the more accurate the sounds become.

Each sound card provides a picture of an item that makes the sound associated with it. The item in the picture itself does not necessarily begin with the sound – the focus is on the sound that is made by the activity illustrated in the picture, for example, the sound of water going down a plughole (g). Most of the sound pictures are within children's daily experience, such as a ball (b), a drum (d), a lady singing (l), a balloon coming down (f), the wind blowing through curtains (h), a tap dripping (t) and so on. Some are not, such as a pea popping, although children quickly learn all of the cards as a part of the game.

Speech and language development for infants with Down syndrome

> **A guide to typical speech sound development**
> - Age 2 years: m b p h w
> - Age 3 years: k g t d n ng f
> - Age 5 years: s z l v y th sh ch
> - Age 6 years: r j

> **A guide to speech sound development for children with Down syndrome**
> - Age 2 years: p b d m n k w
> - Age 3 years: l r s t j g f z sh h v - some blends
> - Age 4 years: ng th ch

First consonants

Twenty of the 23 consonant sounds on the checklist are represented in the DownsEd sound cards. The pictures are chosen to represent the sound - that is the *sound* made by the object in the picture is the target sound.

Vowels

Nineteen of the 21 vowel sounds on the checklist are represented on the DownsEd vowel sound cards. The pictures are chosen to represent the sound - that is the *sound* made by the object in the picture is the target sound.

Development of sounds

As an approximate guide, the ages by which children (90%) can produce the single speech sounds accurately are listed below, based on typically developing children who do not have Down syndrome or language delay. Among all children there is very wide variation, and the order of development of sounds cannot be predicted for individuals.

For all children, spoken words become more intelligible with increasing age and use of their language skills. Achieving intelligibility takes time, even for children who do not have specific speech and language disorders or delays. Studies suggest that at 2 years of age, 25% of children are intelligible, at 3 years, 70% and at 4 years, 90%. This does not mean that all the four year olds can pronounce all their words as clearly as adults but it does mean that 90% of them speak clearly enough to be understood by an unfamiliar adult.

A study by Libby Kumin and colleagues in the USA[6] provides some guidelines to the expected speech progress of children with Down syndrome.

The reader may note that many of the sounds are not delayed in this study and are being learned in a different order when compared to typically developing children. The children in this study were receiving intensive speech and language therapy and not all children mastered all of these sounds. There was great variation between children, with some children having clear early sounds at 2 years and others had not mastered the same sounds at 6 years.

Many of the early difficulties noticed in children with Down syndrome are part of a normal process, and will improve, provided the children have sufficient practice through talking and using their skills. The children may be able to say a sound on one day and not the next and more practice and feedback over many months may be needed to establish consistent production. Early attempts at words may not even be close approximations and so any attempt should be rewarded.

Please notice that some sounds are not accurately produced by many 5 years olds who do not have Down syndrome or language delay. Learning to say sounds may be slow, including the progression from being able to make the sound after it has been modelled and being able to produce it from memory without a prompt.

While lack of confidence can contribute to slow progress, it is more likely that an unresponsive child *cannot remember* the sounds without a prompt, even though he/she may recognise it when it is said and can imitate it, rather than he is she is being deliberately resistant to producing the sound. When children understand what the game is, most will say the sounds they know and can say, in a positive and enjoyable learning situation.

Speech and language development for infants with Down syndrome

Never let your child feel that they have disappointed you or place them under pressure to produce sounds or words.

Remember that making sounds spontaneously during babble and play is a different and easier task than producing a sound on request or in imitation. Similarly, imitating sounds and producing sounds without prompts to imitate, are different skills. The more children use their sounds in play and in games with sound cards the more they are helped to progress through these stages. Having fun with sounds gives children the building blocks for when they start to talk. Practice through listening, watching, imitating and trying to say, will help to teach your child how to produce sounds and, later on, to say words.

Sound practice beyond sound cards

Letter sounds

As children progress in their language knowledge and skills and get older, it becomes appropriate to move into alphabetic systems of representation by teaching letter sound recognition. This will help to link their speech and language activities to their developing literacy skills. The majority of children with Down syndrome are likely to begin to learn letter sounds between 3.5 to 5 years. The groups of children participating in the Early Development Groups at The Down Syndrome Educational Trust in this age range have continued to enjoy using the familiar sound cards they know and have practised for several years, as well as to learn letter sounds and play letter sounds games. The two methods for facilitating speech sound practice have not confused the children.

Although most children beginning this type of work at school age can skip the sound cards and commence their sound practice by learning letter sounds, some children with very little speech who are still experiencing difficulties with single sound production may find it easier to get started with sound cards. Vowel sounds in particular may need picture alternatives to letters to facilitate practice.

Computerised systems are also available as a complementary way of enabling children to practice sound production, for example, *SpeechViewer III*.[7] This laptop computer version provides visual feedback so that even young children (3 to 4 years), and certainly older children (7 years and above) can see how close they are getting to making a sound accurately. When they have made the right sounds (or series of sounds, or pairs of sound contrasts like 'sh' and 's') they are visually rewarded for doing so. There are visual incentives that help to speed up the saying of single sounds in a series of repetitions, for example, with a frog jumping from lily pad to lily pad, every time a sound is said. *SpeechViewer* also has facilities for encouraging many other aspects of speech development, as well as phonology, including voice, pitch and control of breathing.

Figure 3. Animal Cards
These can be used to play 'What is it called?' and 'What does it say?' In a group, one child can select a card from the set and name the animal, and the next child can give the sound.

Figure 4. Sound Bubbles
Place the cards face down, ask the child to select a bubble. The child then turns it over and makes the sound. In a group game, if the snake is found everyone makes the 'sss...' for snake noise. The bubbles illustrated can also be used to name the colours for another game.

Speech and language development for infants with Down syndrome

Improving sounds in words

Once children have begun to speak, they are practising sounds in words all the time. For example, even in the first 100 words that children typically use, almost every consonant and vowel sound is used. Initially children's sounds in the words will be approximations, determined by their phonological and speech production skills. For children beginning to learn to speak, we would not expect consonant clusters ('dr' as in drink, 'tr' as in train, or 'sp' as in spoon) to be used, or even two consonants in a word, and many words will be recognisable to parents by the vowel sounds, context, use of sign. At this stage, the addition of one consonant somewhere in the word is good progress.

The 120 words on the first vocabulary checklist are used daily in most young children's worlds and by practising these, children are developing their sound systems. Of these 120 words, about 20% begin with a 'b' sound, with 12% beginning with a 'k' and 10% with a 't' sound. About 6% begin with 's', 'd', 'h' and 'w', 4% with 'p', 'm', and 'f', 2% with 'l' and 'sh', and 1% with 'y' and 'v'.

For the final or second consonants of the words, 17% end with 't', 15% with 's', 10% with 'n', 9% with 'k' and 'g', followed by 'l', 'd', 'r', 'sh' and 'b' in decreasing order.

For vowel sounds, the most commonly used in these words are 'a' as in 'bag', 'oh' as in 'boat', 'i' as in 'big', and 'u' as in 'bus', followed by 'o' as in 'sock', 'ee' as in 'eat', 'ay' as in 'wave', 'oo' as in 'spoon' and 'eye' as in 'light'. Other vowels used are 'ow' as in 'cow', 'e' as in 'bed', 'au' as in 'ball', 'a' as in 'want', 'ah' as in 'car', 'u' as in 'book' and 'look'.

Add to this, the complexity of the order in which the sounds occur and the changes in position of the speech muscles to sequence the sounds in the word and it is easy to understand why children omit consonants at the beginning or end, or both, especially in two and three syllable words. More positively, any amount of talking, even with very first words, will enable practice of the whole range of sounds needed for speech.

Repeating the words that children say so that they can hear them correctly spoken, and encouraging them to speak in games and through interactive play, with feedback, will develop their speech clarity. Be careful not to criticise though, as this may discourage your from child speaking. Repeating single words back on every occasion may distort the flow of conversation; so try to feed back the correct production of a word in a natural way. If words lose their communicative value, and the focus is totally on clarity of production in all situations, this could have a reverse effect and lead to the word being practised less. For example, when a child has asked for a ball you might say, "yes, let's find the **ball**" (emphasising the word the child said, clearly and quite loudly) or "**park**, that's right, we are going to the **park**" (again emphasising the word).

When children talk and are given feedback through interaction, they will continue to develop their phonological system and improve their speech. This is likely to be accelerated when they have been introduced to literacy teaching and if they are in a good language learning environments at home and school.

But, for the majority of children with Down syndrome ordinary communication experience alone is not sufficient to lead to the development of clear, intelligible speech in later years, and they can be helped to progress more quickly by focused practice on single sounds, series of single sounds, series of varied sounds, sounds in words, pairs of words with contrasting sounds and additional practice for joining words together in longer combinations.

Practice sessions that are focused on improving phonology and speech production have an advantage to practice during everyday communication, in that the child and parent both know that the game is about how you say the word and it focuses their attention on phonology. When a word can be said in a practice session, then it can be generalised to everyday language, with activities designed for this purpose.

Choosing sounds and words to practice

In order to speak clearly, children have to be able to say single sounds, then to join sounds together in a variety of ways to produce clear words of one or more syllables and finally string words together to produce sentences. At each step, the speech-motor planning and control required increases. Most children with Down syndrome will be helped by activities for each stage – at the sound level, the word level and the multi-syllable, multi-word or sentence level.

For young children in the early stages of speaking, who are not able to produce the full range of sounds, and children who are finding it very difficult to speak who are a little older, words that contain sounds that they can say can be targeted for practice, as these are more likely to be achieved. You can use the vocabulary checklists with this module to choose words to try with them.

Speech and language therapists are able to listen to children's speech or look at records of words they can say, and make suggestions for therapy, to move them forward gradually and with success, without asking them to say words that are just too difficult at that stage in their speech development. Of course children need to practice difficult words and phrases too, and need to be gently encouraged to do so all of the time, but targeting a set of words closer to their current skill level will help them to be successful and to gain in confidence.

Without a speech and language therapist to help guide and structure the practice, we advise parents to use the speech sounds and vocabulary checklists to guide the selection of sounds and words for practice and to record progress. The sound list will help you to choose sounds for sound games and the word lists indicate words that your child can attempt but not yet say clearly.

Games with individual sounds

Practising with individual letter sounds in games, and speeding up a child's ability to accurately produce sounds is good practice for all children. Some children will still need vowel sound practice, so use vowel picture cards or combine letters in your language that usually make that sound, ideally with a character or visual reminder as well, or you can choose words that contain the vowel sounds (eyes, ear, mouth, nose, and animal sounds, baa, moo, etc). Practise letter sounds you are working on (not too many at once) and also practice words (with pictures) beginning with the same letter sounds as a complementary activity. Do not wait for all consonant and vowel sounds to be achieved before practising words, but choose words that contain some of the sounds your child can say.

Practice words that are important to the child and will help her/him gain some control over daily events. Words that your child wants to use to request and comment will be learned the fastest. Next, choose topics of interest to expand vocabulary such as the farm, animals, or – for older children – a project in progress in the classroom.

Various 'ladder' games (like those illustrated overleaf) made with pictures and letters can be used to encourage children to practice single sounds repetitively, and the same technique can be used for whole word practice or contrasting word practice. Large clear ladders with characters that physically jump up the ladder rungs can be used for young children, as well as letters that jump across markers on a table or grid into a bag or to be eaten by a glove puppet. Where children are familiar with formal work, printed ladders of various types can be used, for letters or words, as illustrated below for the word 'dog'. The stickers on this example were awarded, as the child was able to complete each stage for the first time.

Choose words with one letter sound targeted in one position

For example, choose a list of pictures and words that all begin with 'b'. Work through groups of words beginning with different letter sounds that you are targeting for practice. Picture resources or books that have vocabulary items listed alphabetically are useful for this, as you will already have child-interest words all beginning with the same sound presented together. Please note that clusters such as 'sl' or 'tr' need to be practised separately and are not suitable for practising the single sounds 's' or 't'.

At this stage you will know which sounds in words, at least in the initial position, are difficult or easy for your child to say, as well as how easily he/she can say sounds in isolation. You might chose to put a difficult word in with a list of easy words for your child to practice, to encourage them, and as you get more practised and your child more confident, you can choose words that really target your child's particular difficulties. If you listen to your child carefully, you will notice what some of their difficulties are, but you will need to break up words and design activities that are at the easiest level you can think of, and that you can build up later on, so that practice items are not so difficult that they are discouraging for the child.

Joining sounds for words and syllables

Joining one consonant to one vowel, as in 'key' or 'see', is easier than saying words with more sounds in them (cat, brick, slip) or a multi-syllable word, where many changes in position of the tongue, lip and soft palate are needed to make the word. (The soft palate closes so that air does not go down your nose, as in 's' and 'sh' words, and opens so that it does come down your nose a little, when you say 'm' and 'n'). Words with one consonant, like 'Emma' are easier than 'packet' with two consonant positions, or 'snail' or 'school' with consonant clusters at the beginning.

Make a list of words your child can say clearly and see what similarities there are – in vowel and consonant type and position. Can he/she imitate two or three syllable words? Children's progress will be affected by how difficult it is for them to make each single sound. The easier this is for them, the more likely they can move from one sound to the next to join the sounds swiftly

Speech and language development for infants with Down syndrome

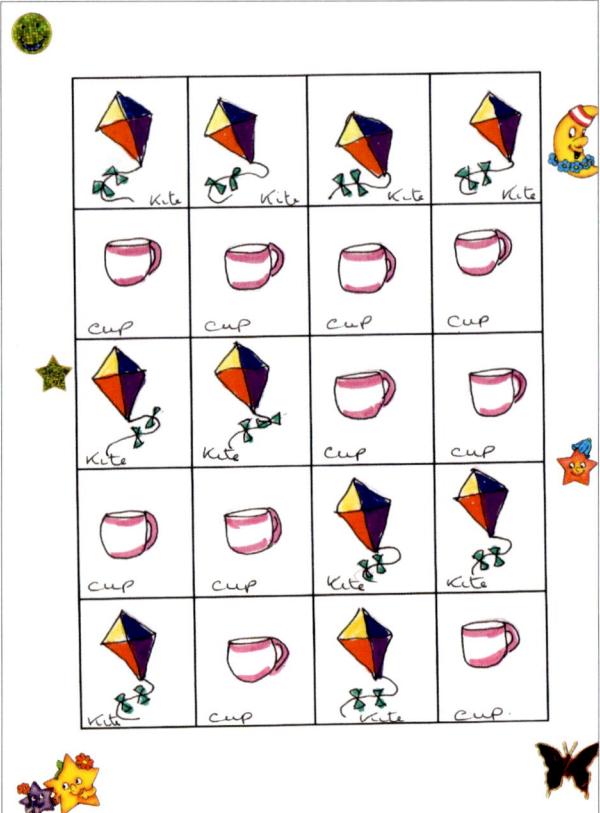
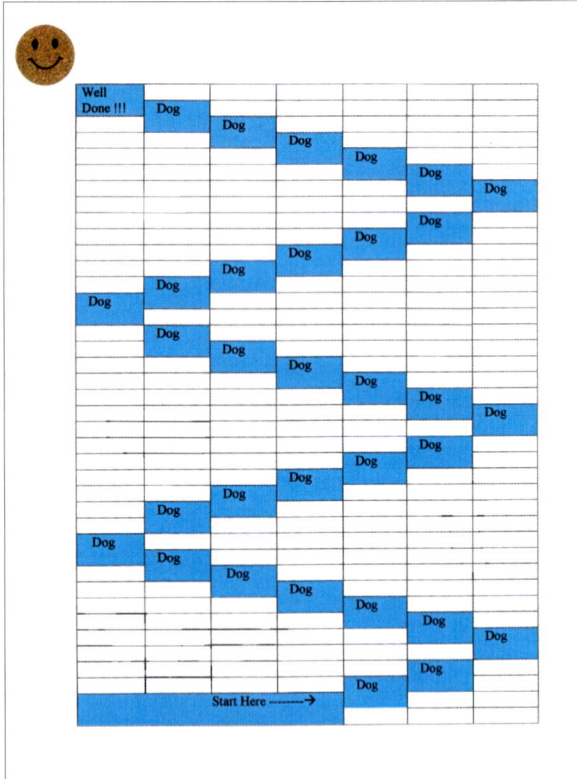
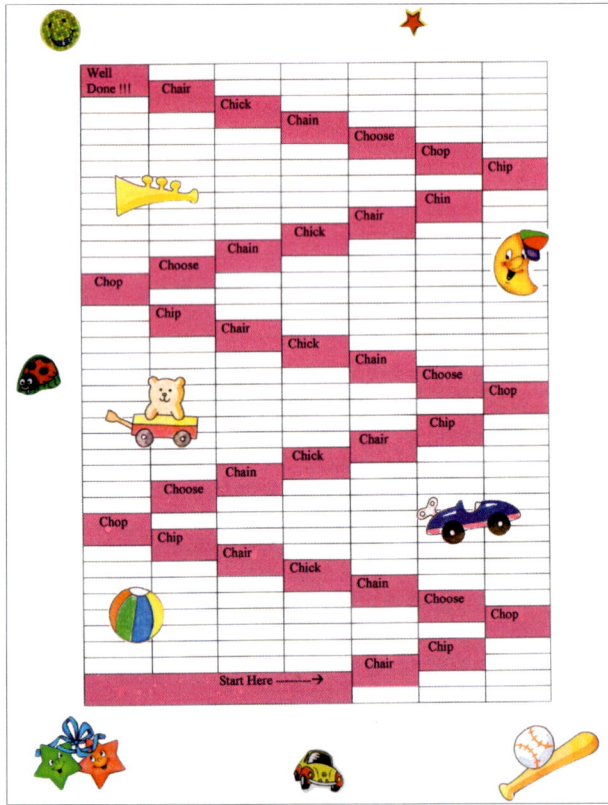

Figure 5. Examples of games to make for sound practice
The top two examples illustrate contrasting pairs: The child has to work along each line saying the words. The lower two examples illustrate ladders to climb: The child 'climbs' the ladder, pointing to each rung of the ladder and saying the word. These are fun games which can be made with any words to encourage speech practice.

enough to make a word.

For focusing on the production of the rest of the word, after the initial sound, choose words where your child can say the initial sound, and that have a different ending, as illustrated in the example below for 'bun' and 'bus'.

Although choosing sounds and words to practice seems and is quite difficult, we usually expect children to learn how to say them just from listening to the words around them, without any structured help. Some selection of words that they are already trying to say, and defined practice activities, will make the task easier. Do not be too worried about 'doing it wrong'. Make sure the tasks are fun and designed to help your child to achieve the next step – if they can't, do more practice at an earlier step. Ideally, you will have a speech and language therapist who can help you. When practising two or three syllable words, encourage your child to tap out the number of syllables, in order to focus their attention on them.

For practising words, one way of deciding what is close to being achieved is to identify what words the child can imitate but is unable to say clearly without a model to copy. The vocabulary checklists provide a column for you to record these words. Successful imitation indicates that the child can physically say the words and the sounds in the words, but has not yet said them enough to remember how to say them spontaneously. With some extra practice, they will learn to do so.

Important words, words that children need, words that are likely to be practised every day

Another approach for choosing words to practice to improve children's production is to choose words that the child needs or wants to say, and practice these. For example, most children at school, will need to say number words, and will be practising every time they count. They will need to say the names of members of their family, or pets names, their teacher's name and title (Mrs Xxxx), where they live, how old they are, etc., to request their favourite activities, or asking simple questions that can get them more information or aid their communication (help please?, my turn), and the more they practice the better they will get. With this approach parents will need to be very accepting of every effort, as some words will be very difficult for some children, even though they are motivated so say them. You may need to break words down into smaller parts and practice these, and of course break sentences down into words to practice in turn (just as you do when reading word by word).

Targeted practice can help at any stage or age

Children who talk fairly well (or are considered to, compared with other children with Down syndrome) will still benefit from these types of activities to improve their speech clarity, and some examples of more advanced words are included for this reason, for example 'ch' words and 'str' words.

Joining words together

Joining words together is more difficult than saying single words on their own, and it is typical for children's clarity to fall back a little when they try to do this. But with practice they get better, although they should be able to say the single word clearly before they are expected to say it clearly in a sentence. You can build up two, three, four and five word sentences, practised

---

Facilitate practice by

- Encouraging your child to listen, imitate and try words.
- Engaging in games, play or real activities to use the target sounds and words
- Including the targeted words learned in everyday language, so that the child can use the words they have practised and hear you using them for real.
- Using visual supports, pictures, letters, words, objects, books etc to support practice or sounds, words and sentences.
- Using quality materials - colourful, interesting, well made (mounted, laminated) pictures that the child can handle are far more likely to hold children's attention and be used than black and white photocopied line drawings on thin paper.

with visual prompts, like words and pictures, with a model to copy, which help children to focus on their pronunciation.

Features of successful therapy programmes for improving phonology

Of the few evaluated and published therapy programmes, one that dramatically improved the phonology of young children with Down syndrome, aged between 4 and 6 years at the start of the programme, provided weekly or fortnightly therapy from a speech therapist, with a 20 minute practice session by parents daily when possible, over input periods of 4 to 6 weeks followed by breaks of 4 to 10 weeks. This study, by Clothra Ni Cholmain,[8] monitored changes that occurred through the training programme.

The programmes were individual according to each child's skills, but each shared the following key features:

1. Listening

The child listens to lists of words read to them by the parent for 6 to 10 minutes every day, with the help of a portable amplifier.

2. Production

The child is asked to produce some of these words (chosen from those they could imitate) with the child saying the words into the portable amplifier. Guidance was provided for parents to include these same words in everyday games and activities, such as picture lotto and a shopping game. Parents were encouraged to request that the child repeat or clarify the target words, by expressing uncertainty about what the child had said.

3. Sound practice

Sound cards or books were provided for the children, which contained picture symbols both for phonemes being targeted and those already in the child's system. They were used to encourage the children to think about speech sound as sounds, and provided opportunities for listening and production practice in play.

All of the 6 children who participated in the programme showed change in their phonological systems within the first two weeks and appeared to begin to reorganise their phonological and sound production system.

Remember that the activities for encouraging all aspects of speech and language development will also help speech clarity, and that the more children speak and listen the more they will improve in their speech production. Children with severe hearing loss are greatly disadvantaged for learning to speak clearly and treatment with hearing aids is vital. Consider how you can practice and improve clarity of speech through play, using the activities described as useful for developing vocabulary comprehension and speech, through everyday conversation and through reading activities.

For activities and games that break speaking tasks down, for graded practice with pictures, words and letters, please refer to the box (right).

Teaching vocabulary

These guidelines for choosing vocabulary are based on the principles used in vocabulary teaching studies reviewed in the overview module.[DSii-03-01 p.28] They have been successfully used with children with Down syndrome, late talkers and children who have had hearing difficulties due to middle ear

> **Graded practice**
>
> - Listening and repetition of single sounds (s, p, v,)
> - Listening and repetition of a consonant and a vowel (boo, bee, moo, mee)
> - Listening and repetition of a series of single sounds (f,f,f,f,f,f,f)
> - Listening and alternation of two sounds (try two sounds in similar mouth positions first, like p - b, or p - t then gradually get more difficult).
> - Listening and repetition of words – repeat one word, or repeat a list of words/pictures with the target sound at the start of the word
> - Alternation of word (picture) pairs with contrasts or differences in a part of the word (e.g. pea, tea)
> - Listen and imitate verb list, verb plus –ing, 2 syllables, pictures, clapping or tapping out
> - Listen and say sound clusters, with letters on card (e.g. sl, sk, sn)
> - Listening and repetition of words that begin with targeted clusters – same word or mixed words
> - Alternation of three sounds (e.g. p,t,k, or three vowel sounds, or mix - consonant, vowel, consonant)
> - Alternation of more difficult word pairs
> - Words with similar word ending e.g. single syllable words with 't' at the end
> - Build up syllable practice, 2 syllable words, 3 syllable words
> - Single word practice for words in the order they will be joined together, with pictures, symbols and words

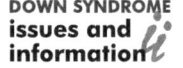

problems (otitis media) similar to those commonly experienced by children with Down syndrome.

While vocabulary is being learned during everyday learning opportunities at home and at preschool, children with Down syndrome need more structured help to support their learning, using modelling (you name the object, picture, event or action) and imitation (you encourage your child to repeat the word with you).

Choose two sets of words, one set for **comprehension** activities from the words that your child does not yet understand and one set for **production** activities from words that your child understands but does not yet say.

Choosing vocabulary to teach

First complete the appropriate vocabulary checklists to identify the words that your child understands and the words that he/she uses in speech or in sign and complete the speech sounds checklist. (Start with Vocabulary Checklist 1 even for an older child, just to be sure that he/she does understand and use all these early words, and then Checklist 2). Choose to work with words that you feel your child will be interested in and that you can use naturally in play or daily activities – or by making a topic book.

Choosing comprehension targets

From the checklist, choose 5 words that your child does not yet understand and that you think that he/she will be interested in learning. As your child learns to understand the words on the list, mark their success on the checklists and choose new words to work with.

Choosing production targets

From the appropriate checklist, choose 5 words that your child understands but does not yet say. Choose words that start with sounds that your child can make or attempt to make. As your child learns to say the words on the list, mark their success on the checklists and choose new words to work with.

You may find that it is helpful to put the words up in the kitchen or on a noticeboard to remind everyone in the family to help you to use teach the words.

These lists of target words will help you to make a planned effort to extend your child's vocabulary, but you will also be teaching them other new words during your daily talk with them at home and at school, so remember to update the checklist by reviewing it from time to time. If you keep a notebook handy you can note down words that your child is saying and understanding as you observe them.

Games for vocabulary learning

All sorts of games can be played to support vocabulary learning, including finding, matching and sorting real objects, doing the same with picture cards and learning from picture books. These activities provide the opportunity to give children many more opportunities of hearing a word and associating it with the correct meaning than will occur naturally during the course of the day.

The natural opportunities for drawing the child's attention to the language being used in every day interactions are equally important. Speak clearly

Speech and language development for infants with Down syndrome

to children at all times, describing what they are doing or interested in and involving them in the conversation.

When teaching vocabulary, remember to teach some verbs, adjectives and pronouns as well as nouns. If a child only has nouns, i.e. names for people and things, he/she cannot move on to put two words together. Two word combinations need nouns plus an adjective or verb – 'red car', 'big car', 'car gone', 'baby sleeping'. At the two-word stage, symbolic play activities can be a good way to introduce more verbs, adjectives and prepositions, and to use them in two and three word combinations. For example, home games with dolls and teddies provide opportunities to 'give dolly a wash – cuddle - drink', 'put dolly to bed – on the chair – in the pram'. Try taking turns with the child, so that he/she can have fun asking you questions and giving you instructions.

Remember that comprehension comes before production, especially for children with Down syndrome.

It is very important to continue to expand the number of words that children understand even though they cannot say them if we do not want to hold back cognitive development, that is world knowledge, thinking and reasoning and remembering.

The child's understanding can be checked by asking them to choose the right picture or object from a choice of items for verbs and adjectives, place things correctly for prepositions and act out themselves or with toys for verbs. It is important to proceed at the child's pace and to be sure that he/she is really understanding and responding at each step. Plenty of fun repetition from playing games, singing rhymes and reading stories will help the learning process.

Comprehension and production of language

- Children understand spoken language before they use it
- Therefore, children's understanding of language should be assessed separately from their spoken language skills
- Spoken language skills are referred to as production or expressive language skills by researchers and speech and language therapists
- Understanding of language is referred to as comprehension or receptive language knowledge

Matching, selecting and naming

Teaching games that use matching, selecting and naming activities, with real objects, toys or pictures, are a very effective way to teach new words and concepts. These activities can be used for many years to teach new words and concepts such as colours, shapes and numbers.

Matching – This simply involves having two identical objects, words or pictures and showing your child how to *find the one the same* though we would not use that instruction at first. We would say "can you put the ball with the ball" or "the shoe with the shoe" and help the child so that they get it right while they are listening to and learning the words. Most children with Down syndrome soon understand and learn to match pictures between 18 and 24 months.

Selecting – the next step is to ask you child to select the picture or object that you name, for example, "can you give me the ball", "can you show me the shoe". When he/she can do this you know that they now associate the word that they are hearing with the right object – they understand the word.

Naming – the last step is to ask the child "what is this" or "what's this called" as you point to an object or picture. The child can respond with a sign or a word, though you should *always say the word*.

Your child will progress from matching, to selecting and then naming, maybe taking several weeks at each stage when starting to learn words. He/she will be able to show you, by selecting, that she/he understands many more words than he/she can name, during the preschool years.

Speech and language development for infants with Down syndrome

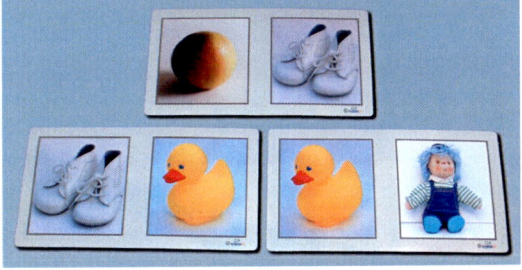

Figure 6. DownsEd Picture Dominoes cards

We have designed two early games for matching games (*DownsEd Picture Lotto* and *Picture Dominoes*) using large cards and pictures from the First Vocabulary list, to help you to teach matching, selecting and naming. You can then move on to the Lottos which are available in toy shops. The DownsEd Language cards illustrate 55 of the words on the first vocabulary checklist. The booklets with these games contain instructions for games and activities to play with the cards. The Language cards can be used to move onto two-word phrases and to introduce reading.

We recommend that you use real objects, toys and pictures to teach vocabulary. We discuss the use of symbols systems later but most children with Down syndrome do not need to be introduced to picture symbol systems – they will learn in the ordinary way from everyday experiences, play with toys, pictures and picture books. However, if you have a child who is particularly delayed and having difficulty in learning words, then the use of symbols may help her/him to communicate. Like signs, symbols need to be used with thought and with planning, based on individual needs, and not used indiscriminately and certainly not just because your child has Down syndrome. This applies to their use in school as well as at home. Many symbols have no advantage over pictures, which occur in the everyday environment and in books. Other symbols have to be learned, their meaning is not obvious, and at this point you are teaching another 'system' to be learned (rather like teaching

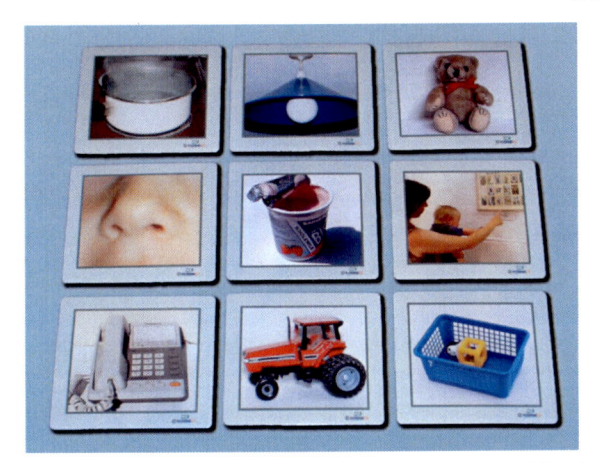

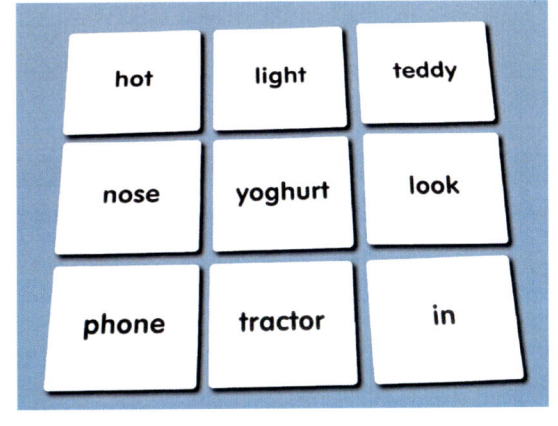

Figure 7. DownsEd Language Cards, front and back

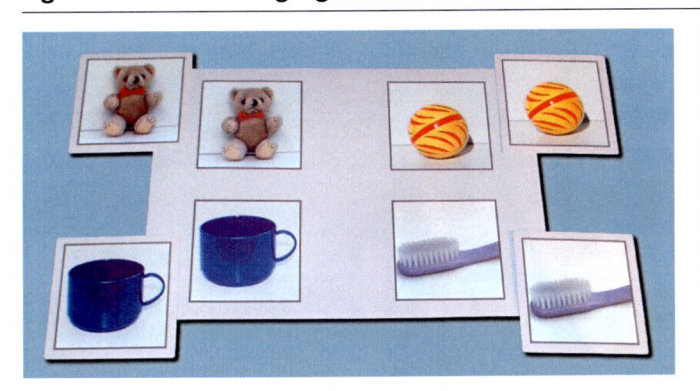

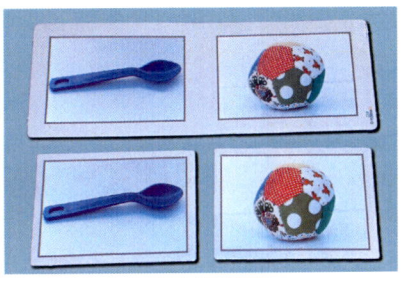

Figure 8. DownsEd Picture Lotto cards

Chinese symbols) and you need to be clear why this is helpful and why you are not moving straight to printed words if you need a visual language.

Teaching first words

Importance of mixed vocabulary

Children need to be able to use a variety of single words before they begin to join two or more words together. For example, as well as naming objects and people, they need to be able to understand and use a variety of different action words (verbs); sleep, wash, eat. They also need to be able to use social and greeting words; hello, good-bye, yes, no, more, again.

> **When teaching words:**
> - Remember to make all of the activities fun
> - Take turns at the game to show your child the correct response
> - Prompt your child, if necessary, to ensure success
> - Do not create anxiety, pressure or a 'lesson' atmosphere

In this section on teaching single words, the first part deals with specific activities, for comprehension and expression of the different types of naming, action, social and greeting words. The second part discusses doll play and the final part deals with utilising daily activities for language, teaching and learning.

In the first part some activities may have been suggested for teaching the names of objects and for teaching clothes and food names but the same activities can often be used for teaching other categories of words.

When you play these games, it is important to join in the game and to take turns with your child or a group of children. Set up a routine so that your child is familiar with the sessions and ready to engage. Support your child to play the game, prompting correct responses to encourage learning and avoid failure. Model the successful responses, take turns and make it fun. Try not to create a 'lesson' atmosphere, which may create anxiety and pressure for your child.

I. Teaching nouns - names of objects

Comprehension games

Gather together a box of common objects, e.g. cup, car, keys, brush, flannel, toothbrush, book, shoe, brick, ball, pen, spoon, plate, etc. (increase the choice of objects as the child shows he understands these verbal labels). Show the child each item and say what it is called as you place it on the box or on the table.

(a) Place six objects in a box with a lid. Show the child inside the box and then shut the lid. Now ask the child to "find the car". Either open the lid yourself or let him/her open it and find the object and remove it.

(b) The same as (a) but use a large bag instead of the box to make a change.

(c) When sitting at table, place some objects (say 3-6) in front of the child and ask her/him to "give me the ball".

(d) Choose several large objects and put them in prominent positions around the room while the child is looking. Then ask her/him to "bring me the car". Your child has to go to the object and bring it back to you.

(e) Names of furniture can be taught by giving the child something and asking him to "put it on the table" or "on the chair" or "on the bed".

(f) Picture lottos can be a good way to teach words, especially if they have realistic pictures, as you can start with matching games. Ask your child to "put the picture of the apple with the apple" and help him/her to do this correctly. Children usually get the idea of matching quite quickly and each time they do this you are saying the correct word. Once the child can match the pictures correctly, ask him/her to "give me the apple" or "show me the apple" to test comprehension for the words.

(g) Using picture material may be more difficult for your child but if he/she is interested try cutting out pictures of objects and sticking them on to separate pieces of card. Place three of four on the table in front of your child and ask him/her to "find the ball". This is the *selecting* game described earlier and it can be played with shop bought pictures or lotto cards. The child could then post the picture into a posting box.

Expression games

(a) When you put toys away after a game or get them out for a game, ask your child to name them.

(b) Hide two objects behind your back, putting one in each hand. Hold your hands in front of the child and let her/him choose a hand. Turn your hand over and show your child the object hidden which he/she then has to name.

(c) Put a cloth on the table. Your child has to close his eyes while you place an object under the cloth. He/she then opens his/her eyes and has to find the hidden object and then name it.

(d) Put some objects into a box with a lid or a bag. Your child has to pull out an object with and name it. You can also play a harder version by trying to name the object without looking at it.

(e) Ask your child which toys she/he would like to play with and give her/him a choice; 'would you like the car or the bus?' Encourage her/him to tell you rather than pointing to the object he wants.

(f) Have a selection of objects on your lap. Select one, the child names it and then posts it into a posting box or puts it into another container such as a bag or box.

(g) Picture Lotto. Put the separate cards in a pile and take turns to turn one over, name the picture and match it with the picture on your board.

(i) Using cut out pictures on card, make a pile and take it in turns to turn one over and name - you could win bricks if the word is given correctly, or you could post the card in the posting box. For both comprehension and expression a useful and interesting activity to try is to go through any old magazine or catalogue and cut out different pictures of an object. Then either stick the pictures on to separate pieces of card or into a scrap book. You could try a different object each week or every two weeks.

Names of food

Comprehension games

(a) Always tell your child what he/she is going to eat or what he/she is eating.

(b) When your child has a few different foods on a plate, ask him/her to take a piece of potato or a piece of carrot as the next mouthful.

(c) Make toy food with Plasticine or equivalent and ask her/him to identify the things you have made.

Speech and language development for infants with Down syndrome

(d) Put three different types of food on three different plates and ask your child to "point to the apples", "point to the sugar", "point to the tomatoes".

(e) Let him/her watch while you are cooking and to start with, name the things you are going to put into the dish. Later try asking your child to give you the things which you need.

(f) Talk about things you might eat for different meals, e.g. breakfast, dinner, tea, etc. Cut out pictures of foods, or perhaps draw your own and stick them in a scrap book to talk about at bedtime or a quiet moment.

(g) Pretend to go shopping - have a few packets of food on the table and ask your child if you can have the cereal/bread etc.

(h) If you have any pictures cut out of different foods on separate pieces of card, place three or four of the cards in front of the child and ask her/him to "find the bread" and then post the card into a posting box or give it to teddy who is watching the game.

Expression games

(a) Give your child a choice in selecting food. If, for example, you are offering fruit, show your child an apple and a banana and ask her/him which one she/he would like, encouraging your child to tell you rather than to point.

(b) Ask your child what she/he is eating when she/he is having dinner.

(c) Put three items of food on a tray. Ask your child to name them and then take one away and ask her/him which one has gone. Show your child the one you've taken away if she/he finds this difficult.

(d) Using the cut-out pictures, turn the cards face down on the table (as in the game of Pelmanism). Your child then turns over a picture card and names it.

Names of clothing

Comprehension games

(a) Make a toy clothes line. Choose some clothes, either dolls clothes or babies clothes and put them in a pile with some pegs. Ask the child to find the 'vest', 'sock', etc. Then help him/her to hang them on the line.

(b) Using a mannequin with clothes that you can put on or take off, ask the child to take off coat, trousers etc. and once they are off put them in a pile and ask him/her to put them back on.

(c) The same as above with dressing a doll.

Expression games

(a) Name clothes as you put them on the toy clothesline and encourage the child to name them.

(b) Ask the child which piece of clothing to put on the mannequin or the doll next.

(c) When loading the washing machine, get the child to name the clothes as you put them in or to tell you which ones to put in.

Speech and language development for infants with Down syndrome

Names of body parts

Comprehension games

(a) Sing an action rhyme, such as "head, shoulders, knees and toes", with your child and help her/him to point to his head etc. Then gradually stop doing the gestures with him/her and see if he/she can do them by him/herself.

(b) In the bath give him a face cloth or sponge and ask him/her to wash his face, wash his feet, etc.

(c) In doll play ask her/him to wash his dolly's hands, face, tummy, etc.

(d) Ask him to dry her/his face, etc. after a bath and to dry dolly's face, etc.

(e) Sit in front of a mirror with him/her on your lap and ask him/her to point to her/his eyes, your nose etc.

Expression games

(a) Encourage the child to join in with rhymes (see Comprehension (a)).

(b) Encourage the child to tell you which body part she/he is going to wash and when playing with a doll encourage him/her to ask you to wash dolly's face etc. You say "what shall I wash?"

2. Teaching verbs - action words

Comprehension games

(a) To begin teaching your child simple actions, do the actions together. Play a game where you say "let's run", "let's sit down", let's sleep" and actually do the action with the child. Then gradually stop doing the action yourself and give the child a command.

(b) With a favourite toy ask the child to make teddy sit down or drink or sleep etc.

(c) Sing rhymes involving action words for example, 'Here we go round the mulberry bush'. When you say "this is the way we wash our hands", "this is the way we brush our teeth", "this is the way we run … ", perform the actions and encourage the child to join in. Then gradually stop doing the action yourself and see if the child can do it alone.

Expression games

(a) Let the child take a turn at asking you to run, walk, sleep, etc. It may be a good idea to involve another child or another adult so that you can each take it in turns to make it more of a game.

(b) When your child is playing with a favourite toy, you should have a toy as well and ask the child what you should make your toy do.

(c) Encourage the child to join in with the nursery rhymes.

Figure 9. Pictures to illustrate verbs

Teaching verb particles ('on', 'off', 'up', 'down', etc.)

Although specific activities could be suggested for teaching verb particles, it may be more meaningful for the child if you concentrate on one or two verb particles and try to use them as often as possible in relevant situations throughout the day. If you were concentrating on 'on' you could use it many times throughout the day, e.g. when dressing in the morning "put your pants on, socks on". If you go out "put your coat on" and the same with 'off'. If you choose 'up' to concentrate on then talk about going up the stairs, pick the child and say "up", going up the slide at the park and so on.

Use of social words ('hello', 'goodbye', 'yes', 'no', 'more', 'again')

With this type of word, the times during the day when opportunities for your using the word arise are plentiful and should be exploited. For example, 'more' could be used in brick play if you were building a tower, when you could say "put one more on", or "more bricks". At mealtimes, the child can be encourage to say "more juice", "another biscuit", "another apple", etc. The same applies to names of people in that constant use and exposure to the words will help the child learn their meanings and hopefully encourage him/her to use them him/herself. If you are going to teach the names of animals and you have pets of your own start with their names. Point out dogs and cats as you walk along the road and try and find pictures and perhaps cut them out. Look for models of animals and if your child is able to play with miniature toys use them in his doll play.

Doll play ('teletubbies', 'tweenies', favourite 'doll')

This type of play is vitally important for children to experience, and offers many opportunities to extend the child's understanding and use of language. Playing with toys such as these means that your child can enact everyday situations in a play sequence. *The language you and your child are using is then related to everyday activities and is therefore functional for him.* You do not even need special toys, ordinary household objects (unbreakable!) can be used equally well. You can also use your child's own brush and flannel and perhaps a box for a bed and an old nappy for the doll's blanket.

Listed below are some ideas:

Tea Party

Equipment - dolls and teddies, crockery and cutlery.

Talk about the objects being used and encourage the child to describe what he is doing (action words). Try and follow the child's lead in the activity and avoid imposing too many of your own ideas. However, it may be that your child will initially need more guidance which can gradually be reduced. Describe what the doll and teddy are doing, sitting down, drinking, eating (action words). Describe what they are drinking and eating (names of food). For checking that the child understands dolly and teddy names, you could ask him/her to pass a cup or a plate to the dolly or teddy.

Bath Time

Suggested equipment - washing-up bowl, sponge, flannel, empty shampoo bottle, soap, toothbrush, hairbrush, doll and teddy.

Talk about the objects and encourage the child to use their names. When bathing the doll you can check the child's comprehension of body parts and also whether she/he is able to use the name of any of them. Check her/his understanding and use of verbs like wash, brush, splash, swim. Ask her/him to make the teddy do these. You could also include the use of some social words and perhaps 'more' and 'again' - "Make dolly splash again", "Dolly needs more soap" etc.

Dressing

Suggested equipment - doll and teddy with some clothes.

Here you can use names of clothes and also verb particles because you can put things on and off the dolly and teddy. This kind of dressing play follows on well from the washing play at bath time. You could talk about dolly and teddy getting up out of bed, having a wash and getting dressed like the child would do himself.

Bedtime

Suggested equipment - toy bed (boxes), doll and teddy, something for a blanket, something for a pillow, perhaps a book.

The language you could include in this could be the names of the items listed above and you could use verbs such as sleep, lie down, read, wake up. Talk about putting the dolly and teddy into bed, getting undressed, putting night clothes on etc. Perhaps get the child to show the doll or teddy a picture book and encourage him/her to name the pictures for the dolly.

Using everyday activities for language teaching

Language learning happens throughout the day in every situation. It's important to use simple language and familiar phrases and sign as well if you are teaching your child signs. The following are some ideas on how you can utilise daily routine activities to encourage your child's language development.

(a) *Washing* You could play with a doll at bathtimes and as you wash the child's face he/she could do the same to the doll. Ask the child to wash her/his own face and hands etc. and encourage her/him to tell you what you are washing or perhaps what you are going to wash next.

(b) *Dressing* Place his/her clothes out in the morning and ask him/her to find his/her socks, shirt, trousers, etc. to put on, and once he/she has selected an item correctly, tell him/her to put his trousers on, socks on etc. Encourage her/him to name the items of clothing. Perhaps when you have asked your child to select one, try asking her/him to tell you what she/he is going to put on next.

(c) *Mealtimes* Lay the table, talk about the knives, forks, spoons, plates and ask him/her to put them on the tables, perhaps saying whose spoon it is, e.g. "That's mummy's spoon - put it in mummy's place". Encourage him/her to name the cutlery and tell you where to put it, whose it's going to be. Talk about the food that you eat and encourage him/her to make a choice between items if possible. Use simple language; "eat peas up", "dinner all gone".

(d) *Housework and washing-up* Talk about what you are doing and how you're doing it and encourage the child to describe what you're doing and ask him/her what you're going to do next.

(e) **When on an outing**, point out things of interest and get him/her to talk about them, e.g. if you see a bus, a big bus, a red bus, a cat; if you meet people talk about them.

(f) **Bedtime** When getting undressed, ask which clothes is she/he going to take off, talk about them as she/he takes them off and whether they are going to be washed or worn again. Talk through her/his bedtime routine. Bedtime is also a very good time for having a story!

The importance of books

One of the most valuable activities that you can engage in with any young child, to assist their language learning from the first year of life, is reading books together. Books provide pictures to help you to teach new words and ideas but they also give practice at sentences. As you read even short stories you are using grammatically correct sentences with expression and intonation. Favourite stories are read over and over, allowing your child to learn from the repetition (as they do from favourite games and singing rhymes). Many people who study children's language learning emphasise that children learn language *embedded in familiar contexts* with all the familiar emotions and associations that go with them. We cannot over emphasise this point – it also applies to the language you use at bathtimes, mealtimes, when greeting and so on. The language is learned because it is experienced over and over in situations where the child can *see what you mean*. Stories in books provide another opportunity for learning in a situation of emotional warmth, closeness and sharing enjoyment of the story together. New information and the activities of characters outside daily experience can be shared from books.

Please find time to read with your baby and young child daily. If you can, join a children's library. Children's librarians are experts on the current books available for babies and children of different ages and stages. Here we are stressing the benefits of being read to and listening to language in the context of reading together. Later, we will discuss the benefits of teaching your child to read. Your child will probably have preferences, but it is an idea at first to choose books that are not too long and have clear simple pictures.

You can teach vocabulary from books but do not do this instead of reading the story together or your child may miss out on the pleasure of the story, and the flow of the language as the story is read. Perhaps go back to talk about the pictures after reading the page first. At this point, try asking your child to point to certain objects or to people doing activities. In addition, you could try asking him/her to point to people, events or activities in the pictures. It is also important to give your child an opportunity to initiate speech as well as doing things as directed by you. So as well as asking him/her to name pictures and tell you what people are doing, give him/her space to comment without your direct questioning. Expand any verbalisations. Books are also a way of seeing that they are generalising the language they are learning in other situations and adapting them to this new situation.

Two words

In this section we shall look briefly at encouraging the use of two words together. It is difficult to state an exact moment at which two words or sounds should be expected. When a child has about 50 words is the time to start encouraging him/her to join words together. The Sentences and Grammar Checklist provides a guide to the range of two word combinations

Speech and language development for infants with Down syndrome

Figure 10. Russian dolls
These can be used to teach adjectives such as "big/little" and "tall/short", and later to teach comparatives such as "bigger/biggest" and "shorter/shortest".

Figure 11. Games to teach textures
Collect objects with different textures and put in a bag. Ask the child to feel one whilst saying "What is it?... Is it hard/soft/shiny/rough/smooth..." Take turns to select an item from the bag.

Figure 12. Cars for size or colour
Toy cars collected to teach size and colour: "Can you give me a blue car?", "Can you give me a big blue car?" The man can be used to teach prepositions: "Can you put the man on/behind/in front of the yellow car?"

that children use. Your child needs to be able to use different types of words, not just the names (nouns) that are the first words learned, in order to join words together. The First Vocabulary Checklist provides examples of verbs, adjectives and prepositions as well as nouns, to ensure that you encourage this range of words. As with developing single words, models of the combinations required need to be given. Also the child's understanding must be increasing to the point at which she/he can respond to simple instructions, e.g. "find daddy's coat" (where he/she has a choice of other people's coats or boots) rather than just "find the coat".

Imitation with expansion

One of the best ways to help your child make the transition from the one word to the two-word stage is to use imitation with expansion. To do this you first repeat a word your child has said and then expand what he/she has said, stressing the keywords.

For example, your child may say "car" while pointing to a car and you may respond with "that's *Grandpa's car*" or "it's a *blue car*" or "the *car's going*" as appropriate. Or your child may point and say "dog" and you say "the *dog's barking*", "the *dog's sleeping*" or "it's a *black dog*". One more example might be, your child says "more" and you expand to "do you want *more juice*" or "do you want *more toast*".

Children's early two word combinations often consist of one constant word which they join with many different words, e.g. gone, more, please, by, again, where, in and these are sometimes referred to as pivot words. They are then used with nouns to produce two word combinations such as "more biscuits", "more juice", "more car", "more jump" - "big train", "big shoe", "big coat", "big banana" - "biscuit please", "drink please", "train please", "cup please" - "bye daddy", "bye mummy". Children may wish to indicate possession, e.g. daddy car, mummy bag, dolly foot, or combine the name of a person with an action, e.g. "Billy jump", "mummy go", "baby wash". There may be combinations of an action with an item name, e.g. "kiss doll", "eat please" and so on.

Many of the activities as described in the single word section can be adapted to two words together, e.g. posting pictures or objects into a box. You would ask the child first to put the cup, shoe, brick in the box and then perhaps pick up an object, give it to the child who names it, and then puts it in the box and as he is putting it in the box encourage him/her to say "box" as well so the child begins to say, for example, "cup

Speech and language development for infants with Down syndrome

box", "shoe box" or "in box" or "cup in". You would give the child a great deal of help to start with, gradually reducing the help until he/she can say the utterance by him/herself. You can also play a disappearing objects game. Take an object that is in front of the child away and model "cup gone".

Action words (aiming for name of person and the action)

You could play 'Simon Says'. You say "Simon says 'Billy jump' (or 'daddy hop' or 'mummy sit')". The child is gently encouraged to join in and direct the action using two words. Two word combinations can also be encouraged in doll play. Instead of just asking the child which body part you are going to wash, you could encourage him to use the action word "wash" as well, so that he is telling you to "wash feet" or "wash face" etc. Likewise with the dressing activity you could encourage your child to use combinations such as "coat on", "shoes off", dolly's skirt", dolly's socks" etc. when describing what he/she wants you to do or what you are doing to the dolly. In the tea party situation you could also encourage the use of two words, e.g. when giving out crockery and cutlery encourage the child to say "plate to teddy", "cup dolly", "dolly drink", "teddy eat" and so on.

As with single word activities, there are many opportunities throughout the day for encouraging language development and the situations discussed in the single word section can be adapted so that you use two word combinations, e.g. at bedtime you could, as you are talking about the clothes he/she takes off, say "shoes off", "pants off" and encourage him/her to use these combinations.

In this section, activities have been suggested which can give you an opportunity to concentrate on and work on developing your child's language, both her/his understanding and her/his ability to express her/himself. Many more ideas are listed in some of the books listed in the reference list.[9-12]

Using visual and motor cues

Libby Kumin suggests the use of a *pacing board* to provide a visual and tactile reminder of the number of words your child is trying to use.[9] For example, she suggests that a pacing board may consist of two coloured dots on a piece of cardboard, or two teddy bear blocks put next to each other, or anything else that your child likes. As you use two words point to each spot on the board as you do so. She suggests that helping your child to put their hands on the spots as they say the word will prompt them to recall the number of words that they need and to help them increase their combinations to two, three and four word sentences.

Encouraging your child to continue to sign as he/she speaks may also act as a prompt as they begin to join words. It seems that if they sign each word they may well be able to recall the signs in sequence, and this will act as a prompt for the words that they need. However, remember that at this stage we do not want signs to be used without an explicit reason for them, so you might use signs to model a two word utterance but not use the same signs in other contexts where the child can understand and use the words without help. It will also be apparent that the use of printed words can also help the child to produce multiword sentences.

Speech and language development for infants with Down syndrome

The benefits of teaching reading to teach talking

- Children with Down syndrome have difficulty in learning their first language from listening
- They find learning visually easier than learning from listening
- Printed words seem to be easier for them to remember than spoken words
- Print can be used from as early as two years of age to support language learning
- Many children with Down syndrome can begin to learn to read from this early age and are able to remember printed words with ease
- All language targets can be taught with the aid of written material, even to children who are not able to remember the words and read independently
- Reading activities, at home and in the classroom, teach new vocabulary and grammar.
- Reading enables the child with Down syndrome to practise complete sentences - teaching grammar and supporting correct production
- Reading can help speech at the level of sounds (phonemes), whole word production and sentence production
- Reading to children with Down syndrome and teaching them to read, may be the most effective therapy for developing their speech and language skills from infancy right through school years
- Research studies show that reading instruction in school has a significant effect on language and working memory development for children with Down syndrome

Reading

The teaching of reading and the use of print to support practice should begin once your child understands some 50 words, and can say or sign some of them. They are now ready to understand and use two words together. At this stage we would expect your child to be able to match and select pictures, for example, when playing a picture lotto game, and to name some of the pictures. Your child can then be introduced to learning printed words by playing matching, selecting and naming games (described in Reading and writing development for infants with Down syndrome (0-5 years)[DSii-07-02]).

Researchers worldwide all agree that children with Down syndrome are visual learners. Their visual discrimination and visual memory skills are strengths, while their auditory discrimination and auditory memory skill are a weakness. We have been teaching children with Down syndrome to read from the age of two years for the past twenty years. Progress will vary but many children make surprisingly fast progress and the words that they see in print soon emerge in their spontaneous spoken language. Furthermore, children who start early – at two to three years of age – make the greatest gains in both spoken language and reading skills. They are often reading at an age appropriate level at 8 or 9 years and have very good comprehension and use of spoken language. We would speculate that we may be taking advantage of a period when the brain is maximally open to language learning and that we really are *using print as a way into spoken language for these children*. Please look at the programme described in the reading module and make maximum use of reading to help your child.

Symbols

Picture symbol systems are often advocated for use with children with learning delays and children with Down syndrome. These are often associated with sign systems, but we do not recommend that they are used unless your child is having particular difficulty with learning to talk or to read. We always use ordinary printed words to teach children to read, from as early as two years of age. If properly taught, almost all children will learn the words as easily as symbols. In school situations, placing the word cards around the environment – with picture clues if necessary – will be far more likely to teach children to read than putting symbols everywhere. Like spoken words, the more often a printed word is seen *in a context where you can see what it means* the faster a child will learn and remember it.

If symbols are used in an unplanned way, learning symbols and then print is like learning two languages, like learning Chinese and then learning English. A further problem with the use of sign and symbol systems is that they cannot teach English grammar, unless adapted to do so. Written English is essentially the same as spoken English.

Symbols can be used *to support reading of print* if used in a planned way. Symbols can help to prompt the grammatical words or new words in a sentence and to illustrate topics in an interesting way. Symbols can be used to interest a child in reading, when the child has already experienced failure and is not keen to try reading activities. Then a symbol-supported system, particularly used on the computer, may motivate the youngster because it looks like something new rather than something already disliked.

Three words together

At the next stage your child will be moving to understand and to use three keywords together and examples of the range of three word phrases that children use is set out in the *Sentences and Grammar Checklist*.

As with two word phrases one of the best ways to encourage your child to move on and to string three words together is to engage in imaginative play as already described. Playing games with your child gives you many opportunities for encouraging choices that require comprehension or production of three words or more, such as 'put the cat in the box', 'put the red car on the big box'.

Once your child has comprehension at the three word level, you can encourage expression by playing with your child and getting your child to instruct you to carry out the activities, so reversing the roles of teacher and pupil. Libby Kumin draws attention to carrier phrases such as 'I want', 'I like', 'I see' and identifies that these can be readily taught requiring the child only to add a novel third word.

Prepositions such as 'in', 'on' and 'under', are learned at this three word stage and it is easy to devise games asking children to put something in or on a box or a table or a chair.

Making simple books on a theme such as 'I like' or 'I can' and developing reading activities will help your child to expand the sentences that they understand and use.

Grammar needs to be taught

All the evidence indicates that few children with Down syndrome will learn grammar easily from simply listening to everyday conversations, even though this is how other children learn grammar. The main reason for this may be the slow development of the verbal short-term memory span. Learning grammar involves the processing of sentences rather than single words and this will be very difficult for most children with Down syndrome. There are many ways in which various aspects of grammar can be taught using games but we would argue that reading is the most powerful way to teach sentences and grammar once children have reached a two-word stage in comprehension.

Your child is learning grammar all the time you are talking to them in natural sentences. One simple rule will be effective once your child begins to put two and three words together and that is:

Listen to your child's key words and expand them into the shortest complete sentence. For example "Daddy gone" to "Daddy has gone", "Cat sleeping" to "The cat is sleeping", "Play sand" to "Can I play in the sand, please?", "Mummy go car" to "Mummy has gone out in the car", "Daddy go work" to "Daddy is going to work". You will already be using these expansions naturally (without thinking) as you talk to your child during the day at home or at school. This simple approach will also ensure that you teach using examples that are relevant to your child and will be able to be used by them often when they want to communicate for real.

You can use the same strategy when thinking about making simple books. Words that you wish to teach from the vocabulary lists, such as prepositions and joining words will also give you ideas for sentences to practice in games

Speech and language development for infants with Down syndrome

or with reading activities. For example "Put the book on the table", "The shoe is here not over there", "There is a dog and a cat", "If you get your coat, we can go out", "We need our coats because it is raining".

You can make use of an observation diary to help you observe and encourage your child's grammatical development and ability to use longer sentences. Keep a notepad handy and note down the phrases and sentences that your child is using, both in imitation and spontaneously. This will help you to be aware of exactly how he/she is putting words together and it will help you to follow the guidance on expansion above.

> **Grammar - morphology and syntax**
> - A morpheme is the smallest unit of meaning in the language
> - Bound morphemes are attached to words to alter meaning (such as -ed, -ing, -s)
> - Syntax is the sentence structure or word order rules (for example, for forming a question or a negative sentence)

Syntax and grammar

Grammar can be discussed under two headings – syntax and grammar.

Syntax refers to understanding the way word order changes meaning, for example, "Pat hits Mary" does not mean the same as "Mary hit Pat". Similarly "Daddy has gone to work" changes from a statement to a question if we change the word order to "Has Daddy gone to work?"

Grammar refers to the 'bound morphemes', the word endings that change meaning (for example, 'ed', 'ing' or 's ') and the 'function' or joining words such as 'a', 'the', 'is', 'are', 'if'. The function words seem to be the most difficult for children with Down syndrome, though this is also true for other children with speech and language impairments.

Syntax

Children begin to understand and use word order rules in their 3 and 4 key-word sentences and they then move on to question forms and more complex sentences.

Question forms

Your child will display understanding of question such as "What's that?", "Who is coming?" from quite early, and they will 'ask' questions at the one and two word stage by pointing - but use of question forms in spoken language will come later. Remember to use them as you talk to your child – and to use 'can' and 'will'- "Can you come here please?", "Could you go and look for your shoes, please?", "Will you take this to dad please?", "Will you drink up your juice please?"

It is possible to model questions and answers to encourage your child, for example, "Why are we putting our coats on?... Because it is raining." or "When are we going out?... When Granny comes." In your observation diary, keep a note of the way in which your child 'asks' questions and her/his use of question words. You will also be marking them on the vocabulary lists.

Negatives

As all parents soon find out, from quite early on children understand and use 'no' when they do not want something or they do not want to do something! Children can be helped to understand negatives in a wider range of uses with simple games such as placing objects in a bag, with one odd one out – for example 4 cars and an animal – and saying "Is it a car?" as you take each one out – then "yes, it is a car" or "no, it is not a car, it is a dog".

Picture materials can also be used to teach negatives, for example "He has a hat on", "He has no hat on", or "He hasn't got a hat on". Games to encourage your child to use negatives can be played – "Have you got a hat on?" – and

Speech and language development for infants with Down syndrome

the answer modelled "No, Billy hasn't got a hat on?" This game can be played in front of a mirror, with a hat! In you observation diary, keep a note of the way in which your child indicates negatives and his/her use of 'negative' words. You will also be marking them on the vocabulary lists.

Grammar

When your child has some 250 to 300 words in her/his vocabulary, he/she will begin to use some of the grammatical markers (for example' for plurals or tenses) and more of the function words in their sentences, until they talk in grammatically complete sentences. When you begin to work with Vocabulary Checklist 3, you will use these markers on the words used in sentences.

Plurals

The use of /s/ on the end of a word to indicate a plural is a grammatical rule that is learned early in typical development and simple games can be played to show one or more than one item and use the plural /s/ form. Children with Down syndrome may understand the plural /s/ but not be able to put the /s/ on the words they say because of speech sound production difficulties. There are a number of plural words that are irregular such as feet, and teeth. These just have to be learned and some of the most common ones are in the vocabulary checklists. In your observation diary, keep a note of the way in which your child indicates 'more than one' and the words that he/she is using. You may be marking some of them on the vocabulary lists. When he/she uses the /s/ on words, record this on the Sentences and Grammar checklist.

Possession

The use of /s/ on the end of a word to indicate possession is also learned early. Here again, children with Down syndrome may clearly demonstrate comprehension of the possessive form but not be able to actually sound the /s/ on a word when speaking. They may use possessive pronouns such as 'mine' before using /s/ on words. In your observation diary, keep a note of the way in which your child indicates 'possession' and the words that he/she is using. You will also be marking some of them on the vocabulary lists. When he/she uses the /s/ on words, record this on the Sentences and Grammar checklist.

Function words

Prepositions

Some of the first grammatical words children master are prepositions, such as 'on', 'in', 'under'. Games to teach the meanings of these are not difficult to plan. More difficult pronouns, such as 'beside', 'above', 'below', may not be understood by children of school age. These can be used in sentences and acted out by children in games. In your observation diary, keep a note of the way in which your child indicates 'place' and the prepositions that he/she is using. You will also be marking them on the vocabulary lists.

Figure 13. 'Is it chocolate?' - A negatives game
Put the cards in a bag, or face down on a table, ask the child to select one, saying (for example) "Is it chocolate?... No! It's *not* chocolate it's a key?"

Figure 14. A plurals game
Place the cards face down, ask the child to turn a card. Say "It's two stars/It's one dinosaur. Now watch for another one the same". The child keeps their card while the next participant takes their turn. (This is also a simple memory game).

Speech and language development for infants with Down syndrome

Figure 15. Examples of prepositions games
Ask the child to "Put an animal in/on/under the bag" or ask a child to "Put the man in/on/under the tractor".

Figure 16. Small toys collected to play to 'big/bigger/biggest' and 'small/smaller/smallest' games.

Figure 17. Boy and girl dolls can be used to teach the pronouns 'he', 'she', 'him', 'her', 'his' and 'hers'
For example, ask the child to act out "he is eating" or "she is sleeping". Doll games also give the opportunity to use future and past tenses - for example, "the boy is going to run"/"the girl went to sleep".

Pronouns

Pronouns are a little tricky to demonstrate, especially 'I', 'you', and 'me'. Games played in front of a mirror can help, pointing to yourself while modelling 'I' and helping your child to do the same. Children usually refer to themselves using their own name or 'me' before using 'I'. The use of 'carrier' phrases, such as 'I like......'. or 'I see .....' , and their use in home-made books with photos of your child can help.

In your observation diary, keep a note of the way in which your child indicates 'person' and the pronouns that he/she is using. You will also be marking them on the vocabulary lists.

Articles

The use of the articles 'the' and 'a', and others such as 'some', takes a while to develop. These words, and the auxiliary verbs such as 'is' and 'are', may be difficult because they add very little to the meaning of the sentence. They are also not stressed in normal talk and therefore may be difficult to hear and to process in the flow of words. In our experience, children with Down syndrome do not easily learn to use them in their language and they will be helped by reading them in sentences.

In your observation diary, keep a note of the way in which your child is talking and note down any use of articles. You will also be marking them on the vocabulary lists. When you have heard the use of 'a' and 'the' consistently, tick and date the checklist.

Tenses

There are many tenses in the language, but we have simplified them to present, future and past tenses. To use many tenses properly, an auxiliary or 'helping' verb is used, for example, 'He is going', 'They will be going', 'He has been', 'They are running'. It takes most children with Down syndrome a number of years to master the use of auxiliaries and some individuals never learn to use them. However, most children do learn to use present, present progressive and simple past and future tenses to convey these meanings appropriately.

Children use the present tense of verbs first for example push, jump, sleep, run, and this is the way most of the verbs appear in the vocabulary checklists

Present progressive tense

The next tense children learn is the present progressive 'ing' form, for example, pushing, jumping, sleeping, running. To use this form correctly in sentences they need to use auxiliary verbs - for example, 'I am pushing', 'he is jumping', 'they are sleeping', 'we are running'. You will note that the

Speech and language development for infants with Down syndrome

auxiliaries change with the pronouns (I am, he is, she is, Mummy is) and with singular or plural agents (He is, they are). However children will use the 'ing' form of the verb on its own before they begin to use the auxiliaries. When you hear your child using 'ing' on verbs, tick and date the checklist.

Past tenses

The past tense of verbs comes in two forms, regular and irregular. The regular form is the 'ed' form, for example, jumped and pushed. The irregular forms are all different and have to be learned individually, for example, slept and ran.

A number of irregular past tense forms are learned by children before they use the 'ed' form. Early ones may include broke, came, cut, drank, fell, gave, had, made, ran, sat, saw, took, were, went. A further list of irregular past tense verbs is included in the Sentences and Grammar checklist.

Use of the 'ed' ending

In typically developing children, there is a stage when they seem to realise that 'ed' on the end of a word creates a past tense and they 'over use' it – saying buyed, or goed, for example. In our experience, children with Down syndrome rarely do this but we would be interested to know if you hear your child doing this.

In your observation diary, keep a note of the way in which your child indicates past events and her/his use of the 'ed' ending. In order to use the past tense and to help your child understand, a wall chart for the week or the month can be a great help. Mark significant events on the chart, then you can look at it with you child and say "Yesterday, we went to the park", or "Last week, we rowed a boat on the pond at the park".

There are other past tense constructions such as 'we have been', 'he has jumped', 'he might have jumped before'. We suggest that you leave these to develop with literacy. If at the stage your child is learning to read, you help her/him to keep a simple diary, you will find that you begin to use these constructions.

Children with Down syndrome will understand the language more quickly if the examples used refer to their own activities and actions, rather than to characters in a book - hence the value of keeping a diary.

In your observation diary, keep a note of the way in which your child talks about past events and think of ways to expand her/his own combinations to fully grammatical sentences for practice.

Future tenses

The future tense comes next, but again needs the use of auxiliaries and the verb 'go', for example, "We are going to Grandma's house", "Daddy is going to work on Monday", "You are going to school tomorrow", "he will be going to school tomorrow".

The wall planner for the week or the month will help you to use future tenses and to encourage your child to do so. Mark the future events in the next week and talk to your child about them. As your child gets older, you can extend the planner to cover the year – and teach days of the week, seasons, months, weather – time words, 'tomorrow', 'today' – and time concepts

– 'next week', 'last month' – all with reference to events on the wall planner that your child takes part in.

In your observation diary, keep a note of the way in which your child talks about future events and think of ways to expand her/his own sentences to fully grammatical ones for practice.

More advanced structures

There is a lack of research into the emergence of more complex structures in children's language and even less research on effective ways to teach children to use them. However, the evidence does suggest that both modelling by expanding your child's utterance to the correct sentence and getting your child to imitate by copying you or by reading, are both important strategies. Most children with Down syndrome will be using 3 and 4 keyword sentences by 5 years of age, some will be further ahead than this and some more delayed. Therefore, most children will not use complex sentences until they are in primary school or even later. Young adults with Down syndrome often continue to improve their spoken language through their twenties.

Overview

This module has been written to encourage you, as a parent, carer or teacher, to make a carefully planned effort to accelerate your child's speech, language and communication skills. We hope that you have found the checklists and the games and activities useful and relatively easy to use. We realise that we have provided a large amount of information and have asked you to spend some weeks learning about communication and assessing your child in order to make use of the programme.

We have included this amount of information and detailed guidance because we think it is impossible to exaggerate the importance of speech and language development for every aspect of your child's social and mental development. Please let us know how helpful or difficult that you have found this module and please contact us if you need further help.

What we do not want to do is make parents anxious, therefore, do remember that you are helping your child to progress all day everyday, as you talk naturally to them. Remember to speak clearly and to encourage eye-contact with your child in these everyday conversations. They need to be looking and listening. They will also be helped by visual cues in sign or picture. Remember also that background noise will make listening much more difficult for them if they have any hearing loss. Small rooms help, turn off the TV and radio at home and sit children near the front of the class in school. If you do these things, your child will benefit and if you can use even some of the ideas in this module, then they will benefit a little more.

Speech and language therapy

It is clear that children with Down syndrome will benefit from speech and language therapy from birth to adulthood. In many countries, this will not be a possibility, and parents will need to use these materials without expert help. Parents in this situation might find working together in a small group helpful.

Ideally, in 'developed' countries where these services are available, speech and language therapy should be offered on an individual basis at home in the first months of life, as parents are adjusting to the new baby, and may have many questions to ask. However, in our experience, offering group sessions can be a very effective way to support parents and children in the preschool years. In a group, parents benefit from the opportunity to share their experiences and gain information and emotional support from one another. Group services are cost effective and make good use of professional time, especially as speech and language therapists are often a scarce resource. From 18 months of age, children with Down syndrome are capable of 'working' in a group and they benefit from the social interaction and the models provided by the other children.

The way in which services are offered obviously depends on the availability of speech and language therapists, but ideally a weekly or fortnightly service should be the minimum provided for children with Down syndrome from 12 months to five years of age. In groups, the therapist can model the activities for parents and carers to continue at home. The therapist can also give individual advice to parents or carers. Communication is an all day, every day activity and parents need encouragement and activities to practice, regardless of the rate of progress, so that short courses, such as 6 weekly session, and then a break, is not the best model to use. The aim of expert therapy should be to assist the parents to become the experts, by setting appropriate targets with them for speech, language and communication work, and then modelling effective activities and interactions for them, to enable them to help their child all day, every day, during ordinary daily routines and through planned play and teaching.

It is important that therapists have some specialist training and knowledge of the specific needs of children with Down syndrome, and access to the research literature and appropriate resources. Experience of working with children with moderate to severe learning difficulties is not an adequate basis for working with children with Down syndrome.

References

1. *The Hanen Programme.* Toronto, Canada: The Hanen Centre.
2. Le Prevost, P. (1990). *See and Say.* Stourport-on-Severn, England: TFH.
3. Johansson, I. (1994). *Language development in children with special needs.* London, England: Jessica Kingsley.
4. Passy, J. (1993). *Cued articulation and cued vowels.* Ponteland, UK: STASS.
5. *Nuffield Centre Dyspraxia Programme.* London, England: The Nuffield Hearing and Speech Centre.
6. Kumin, L., Councill, C., and Goodman, M. (1994). A longitudinal study of the emergence of phonemes in children with Down syndrome. *Journal of Communication Disorders*, 27(4), 293-303.
7. *SpeechViewer for Windows* [Computer Software]. (1998). Armonk, NY, USA: IBM Corporation.
8. Cholmain, C. N. (1994). Working on phonology with young children with Down syndrome a pilot study. *Journal of Clinical Speech and Language Studies*, 1, 14-35.
9. Kumin, L. (1994). *Communication Skills in Children with Down Syndrome: A guide for parents.* Bethesda, MD, USA: Woodbine House.
10. Schwartz, S. and Heller Miller, J. E. (1996). *The new language of toys - Teaching communication skills to special needs children.* Bethesda, MD, USA: Woodbine House.
11. Newmand, S. (1999). *Small steps forward.* London, England: Jessica Kingsley.
12. Manolson, A. (1992). *It takes two to talk.* Toronto, Canada: The Hanen Centre.